# INTERLAND

**Previous publications**

**Ralf Andtbacka**
*Öga för öga* (Söderströms, 1994)
*Bikupor om natten* (Söderströms, 1996)
*Café Sjöjungfrun* (Söderströms, 1999)
*En fisk som man kan se* (Söderströms, 2004)

**Steve Dearden**
*if you could count that small forever* (Electric Press, 1998)

**Marko Hautala**
*Kirottu maa* (Porvoon Julmapaino, 2002)

**Kath McKay**
*Waiting for the Morning* (Women's Press, 1991)
*Anyone Left Standing* (Smith/Doorstop, 1998)
*Writing Renewal 2* (contributor) (Government Office for Yorkshire and the Humber, 2005)
A version of 'Stellar Maris' was published by Blinking Eye Publishing, 2005

**Carita Nyström**
*Denna värld är vår* (with Birgitta Boucht) (Boklaget, 1975)
*Ur moderlivet* (Boklaget, 1978)
*Återväxt* (Författarnas Andelslag, 1982)
*Huset i rymden* (Författarnas Andelslag, 1984)
*Vargloven* (Hantverk, 1989)
*Den förvandlade gatan* (Hantverk, 1991)
(in Dutch *Een ander Huis* (Holmsterland, 1995)
*Grönt, grått & rost* (Svenska Konstskolan, 1994)
    (with photographer Pekka Nikrus)
*Galningen i trädgården* (Hantverk, 1996)
*Att öppna en bok* (Hantverk, 1999)
*Brev från en by i Europa* (Hantverk, 2001)

**Adam Strickson**
*Writing Renewal 1* and *2* (contributor) (Government Office for Yorkshire and the Humber, 2003, 2005)
*Stories in a Suitcase* (Kirklees Metropolitan Council, 2004)
*An Indian Rug Surprised by Snow* (Wrecking Ball Press, 2005)
*England Once More (The life, death and unexpected return of Joseph Priestley).* (educational play for Leeds and Philadelphia, filmed and published by the Priestley Society, 2005)

# INTERLAND

Six Steps Underwater
Kuusi askelta veden alla
Sex steg under vatten

Steve Dearden
Kath McKay
Ralf Andtbacka
Carita Nyström
Adam Strickson
Marko Hautala

**Translators:**
Ralf Andtbacka
Marko Hautala
Carita Nyström

*Smith/Doorstop Books*

Published 2006 by
Smith/Doorstop Books
The Poetry Business
The Studio
Byram Arcade
Westgate
Huddersfield HD1 1ND, UK

**Photographs** ©
Dag Ågren
David Collins
Steve Dearden
Tiina Hietikko-Hautala

Copyright © The Contributors 2006
All Rights Reserved

ISBN 1-902382-81-1

British Library Cataloguing-in-Publication Data.
A catalogue record for this book is available from the
British Library.

Designed and typeset at The Poetry Business
Printed by Charlesworths, Wakefield

Distributed by Central Books Ltd., 99 Wallis Road,
London E9 5LN

The Poetry Business gratefully acknowledges the help
of Arts Council England, the Ostrobothnian Arts
Council, and Kirklees Culture and Leisure Services.

POHJANMAAN
TAIDETOIMIKUNTA
ÖSTERBOTTENS
KONSTKOMMISSION

# CONTENTS

*Steve Dearden*

1. Färger / Colour — 12
2. Yta / Surface — 14
3. Sjöben / Sea legs — 16
4. Flak av land / Land Floe — 20
5. Snäcka / Helix — 22
6. Volym / Volume — 26

*Kath McKay*

Stella Maris / Stellar Maris — 30
Floden / The River — 32
Kanalpromenad / Canal Walk — 34
Aska / Ashes — 38
Snö i håret / Snow on our Hair — 40
Simtur / Swim — 40
Simbassänger i Leeds /
 Swimming Pools of Leeds — 40
En kropp / One Body — 42
Det jag minns / What I remember — 44
Jag simmar / I am swimming — 44
Dina bröder ger dig tillbaka
 åt mig i Sydney /
 Your brothers give you back
  to me in Sydney — 46
Haj Känguru Krokodil /
 Shark Kangaroo Crocodile — 48
Fiskar du inte såg /
 Fish You Did Not See — 48
Fjorton veckor / Fourteen weeks — 50
Namn/ord / Names/words — 50
Stinger / After the Stinger — 52
Märken av Australien / Australia marks — 52
Till Phil som har blivit ett träd /
 To Phil who has turned into a tree — 54
Färger i Finland / Colours in Finland — 56
Helsingfors / Helsinki — 56
Ordination / Prescription — 56
Att pejla / Take Soundings — 56

*Ralf Andtbacka*

I – XXI — 60–77
Några noter / Some notes — 76

*Carita Nyström*

Det var en gång / Once — 80
Under ytan / Under the surface — 82
En annan strand / In-between worlds — 84
Simturer / A swim memoir — 86
Vattennyheter / Water news — 86
Ön i havet / The island in the sea — 88
En ö på land / The island on land — 88
Sommarregn / Flood — 90
Orrmoan / Orrmoan — 90
Läsestycken / Readings — 92
I fälan / Seal hunting — 92
Saudade / Saudade — 94
Styx / Styx — 94

*Adam Strickson*

| | |
|---|---|
| Syvyysmittauksia / Depth soundings | 98 |
| Vain sateinen iltapäivä / Another rainy afternoon | 100 |
| Seitsemän kaivon kylä / The hamlet of seven wells | 102 |
| Huone maan alla / A room underground | 106 |
| Toukokuun riitit / Rites of May | 108 |
| Kylmässä helvetissä, tiheikössä / In cold hell, in thicket | 112 |
| Ratsastaa arvoituksen selässä / To ride on the back of a riddle | 114 |
| Kun kuu roihuaa valkoisena / When the moon burns white | 116 |
| Halkaista lasinen jyvä / Splitting the glassy grain | 118 |
| Syöksy / Plunge | 120 |
| Mikä jäi kesken / Picking up | 122 |

*Marko Hautala*

| | |
|---|---|
| 1. Gap / Lovi | 128 |
| 2. She Who Drowns Forever / Aino | 130 |
| 3. Water-Breathers / hiidet | 132 |
| 4. The Grove of Death / Tuonen lehto | 132 |
| 5. Mistress of the North / Louhi | 134 |
| 6. The Mute Creatures of the Cold / manalaiset | 134 |
| 7. The Peasant With a Mitre / Lalli | 136 |
| 8. The Native Land / isänmaa | 138 |
| 9. The Smith / Ilmarinen | 140 |
| 10. The Severed Son / Lemminkäinen | 142 |
| 11. The Lost Spring / kadonnut kevät | 144 |
| 12. Death / Tuoni | 144 |
| 13. The Mother of All Waters / veen emonen | 146 |
| emails | 148–160 |
| illustrated biographies | 162–167 |

# INTRODUCTION

We need to thank some people: the Ostrobothnian Arts Commission and Vaasa Littfest, for the first visit to Finland, which sparked off the collaboration. Also Jane Stubbs and Arts Council England, Yorkshire Office. It was at Jane's house we first talked about water as a theme.

This anthology has been a long time coming. The exchange project between Yorkshire and Ostrobothnia officially started some five years ago, but the seeds were sown even earlier, back in the nineties. In 2004, when the Interland group of writers got together and did reading tours in both countries, we were already writing stuff with the anthology in mind (at least we were supposed to be). Since then, it has been a fairly slow, cumulative process, which is something we quite like. It takes time to digest impressions and to respond to other people's writing on a deeper level.

What we were hoping for from the start was a true collaborative effort, not a collection of separate texts. The contributions in this book, we feel, certainly retain their individual voices, but they are also linked together in significant ways: words and phrases echo here and there, moods and images recur in different texts, ideas and motifs are interwoven. However, when we chose our theme, water, some of us were far from sure that it would work. After all, water is water is water …

But by April 2004 the English crew had met up twice and talked about Finland and swimming, how Kath loves swimming and had written about her journey across Leeds through all the swimming pools. A connection clicked for Adam, a clumsy passionate swimmer, who every summer sets off in search of English sea water warm enough for his determined breaststroke. Steve had been talking about childhood boat journeys to Helsinki and Stockholm, and the movement of the wind sailing a dinghy on chilly reservoirs. At the time, Adam was reading Seamus Heaney's translation of *Beowulf*. There's a passage at the beginning where Beowulf and Breca challenge each other to an epic swimming contest across the open sea. Eventually, Beowulf lands safely on the coast of Finland; he's half swum, half been carried by the waves, worn out from fighting. Our memories blend into each other, but that was when water really began to pull us in.

Adam had an image of descending down the well at the bottom of his West Yorkshire garden, swimming along tunnels and underground rivers, under Leeds, under Goole, out into the North Sea, all the way to Ostrobothnia on the Gulf of Bothnia. We talked about people from colder lands digging holes in the ice and how they let down lines for fish and mysteriously find themselves pulled into the watery underworld of ancient stories. We knew then that we would use the water which separates us and joins us as our inspiration, that we would paddle across cities, sail round islands, stare through the ice, fly underwater, drown and swim. Maybe we'd have some epic fights on the way! We probably also knew then all our work would, in different ways, be submerged in grief and longing.

The Finnish group met several times and during the first sessions there was a lot of discussion, really about everything else but the writing part. Yet it was always there. We had read the first 'water thoughts' sent by the English group and started to get a feel of the theme. So our cue was Beowulf's swimming trip, or, in a wider sense, that special way that myths talk about the past. How they are at once accurate and unreliable, how they mix the actual and fictional.

This led to several ideas: fictional biography, 'travel writing' about your everyday environment, accounts of loss and death, and so on. One could say that these ideas took us further and further from the starting point of watery myth. But, in a way, myth is always about distancing yourself from the immediate, seeing differently, and about loss. Unlike manuals, it talks about things that are not there for you. Things you can't fix or make work for your practical purposes. It is a current that you have to follow.

Beowulf's arrival at the Finnish soil was the perfect image to begin with. It created a kind of backdrop for our project, reminding us that the connections we thought we would have to create have existed long before us.

Beowulf's story begins as someone else's drunken tale. He has to re-tell it from his perspective. Looking at our finished writings, we can see how we have dived into the deepest parts of our own lives and the world of Finland's national epic, the violent and lyrical *Kalevala*, and come up with treasures from the same hoard. Over two years of meetings, readings, emails and occasional drunken tales, we've absorbed each other's thoughts, creating a shared waterscape.

While, in one sense, we never wrote that waterscape 'together', at the translation stage, solving problems, pushing the language, we got to talk about the micro details of life, the tiny differences in words that signify massive differences in things and what we are seeing. The strength of this collaboration was simply spending time together, learning about the three, four, five (more?) apparently similar but very different cultures, exchanging emails, living in each other's weather.

What we liked about the process is that we had time enough to realize how complex any cross-cultural discourse is, even between cultures which are supposedly 'similar'. For instance, at the beginning the UK writers did not really know anything about the dynamics of the language situation in Ostrobothnia, but do now. In these exchanges, there is always a risk of remaining on a very superficial level: you notice similarities and dissimilarities, but do not really let it affect your preconceived views. We got well beyond that level. Reality is always more multifaceted than you expect it to be; recognizing and respecting this fact is the starting-point of real dialogue.

And families. Thinking about what 'got us beyond that level' we recall the rings of family around Interland: partners, children, parents, etc. Don't worry: this isn't going to turn into a

Hollywood thank-you, though the first ring is made up of those people wonderfully alive and who became part of the project, part of getting to know each other. The other ring is occupied by those we have lost, those we have invented, those we have reinvented, exploring their influence, how far we have moved away, how we live beyond them, how we return. Maybe the family is always where difference is most acute and resonance most profound.

And in fact we can add another ring: the extended family of readers, not part of the initial stages, but who are welcome now.

*

*Interland – kuusi askelta veden alla* on kuuden kirjailijan monivuotisen yhteistyön tulos. Antologian teema on vesi, elementti, joka yhdistää historiallisesti kotiseutumme, Englannin Yorkshiren ja Suomen Pohjanmaan. Mutta tekstit luotaavat vettä sen muuntuvissa merkityksissä. Ne ovat yksilöllisiä ääniä, jotka ovat kasvaneet kommunikaatiosta ja yhdessäolosta, kirjoittajien kotiseutujen vaikutteista ja ystävyydestä, joka projektin aikana syntyi. Antologia on kolmikielinen, sillä pohjalaisessa kulttuurissa kuulee sekä suomea että ruotsia. Englanti on ollut projektin työkieli ja sillä on suurin osa antologiassa, jonka julkaisee brittiläinen kustantamo. Toivomme kuitenkin, että tekstit saavat myös suomen- ja ruotsinkielisiä lukijoita.

Lisää tekstien käännöksiä on Interland –kotisivulla osoitteessa www.intland.net.

*

*Interland – sex steg under vattnet* är resultatet av ett flerårigt samarbete mellan sex författare, tre från Yorkshire i England och tre från Österbotten i Finland. Vatten, antologins tema, är det element som historiskt förenar våra regioner, men det har mångskiftande innebörder som texterna dyker ner i. Varje bidrag är ett individuellt uttryck, men är också påverkat av samtal och samvaro, av vår upplevelse av varandras livsmiljöer och av den vänskap som vuxit fram. Antologin är trespråkig, eftersom såväl finska som svenska hör hemma i den österbottniska kulturen. Av naturliga skäl har dock engelska varit vårt arbetsspråk. Engelskan ges också mest utrymme i antologin, som utkommer på ett brittiskt förlag, men vår förhoppning är att texterna ändå ska nå finsk- och svenskspråkiga läsare. Fler översättningar hittas på Interlands hemsida www.intland.net.

**Ralf Andtbacka**
**Steve Dearden**
**Marko Hautala**
**Kath McKay**
**Carita Nyström**
**Adam Strickson**

*Ralf on Steve*

I first got in touch with Steve back in 2000, not long after I had started to work for the regional arts council. Quite a few emails and a couple of phone talks followed, and then we met for the first time in the summer of the following year. Even before I went to England, I felt I had a pretty good idea of what kind of person he was; his personality shines through in writing and in conversation. Right from the start I noticed his intellectual keenness and openness, his attentiveness and his great sense of humour.

On a more professional level, I was impressed by his dedication and knowledge in the field of literature. It was clear that he was driven by a passion for books and writing, and not simply doing a job because it happened to be his job. One word springs to mind: integrity; that quality is present in everything Steve does. During my tenure as Lead Artist in Ostrobothnia, I drew a lot of inspiration from his vision of regionalism in the age of globalization. It was exactly the kind of positive intellectual energy I needed when hatching plans for a literary festival in Vaasa.

Consequently, it was only natural that Steve, along with two other Yorkshire writers, was invited to the first edition of the festival in 2001.

I am fascinated both by Steve's texts and his attitude to writing. There is a strong element of physicality in his handling of language, almost as if words were, literally, a substance that is shaped through the act of writing. In significant respects, in Steve's texts, encoding and decoding reality is a tactile experience or as he writes in the first section of 'Aire': 'All through the grey months I touch my forehead to check I still carry that blue moment inside me.' Touching is a way of actively confirming existence, just as writing is a way of actively shaping reality, or at least one's own understanding of it.

Indeed, literature seems to be an integral feature of Steve's way of being in the world. I have a lot of respect for the way he goes about his writing: there is always focus on the process itself, on producing a good text, rather than on the potential benefits of being a writer, all the useless hype. For him, I believe, literature above all signifies empowerment, intellectually and existentially, and this is the key motivational force behind his work both as a writer and a literary activist.

# Aire

## Steve Dearden

*For Erica Dearden*

    *Tillägnas Erica Dearden*

*Not a big eagle, nor
a little tiny eagle:
one wing ruffled the water
and the other swept the sky
its tail skimmed the sea
and its beak clattered on crags*

*the wind made her womb full
the sea makes her fat*

*water mother : air lass*

    from *The Kalevala*

*Ei ole kokko suuren suuri
eikä kokko pienen pieni:
yksi siipi vettä viisti,
toinen taivasta lakaisi,
pursto merta pyyhätteli,
nokka luotoja lotaisi*

*tuuli tuuli kohtuiseksi,
meri paksuksi panevi*

*Veen emonen: ilman impi*

    citat ur *Kalevala1*

## 1  Färger

Vinterbergen bakom mitt hus svampar ner sig till träsk. Jag håller kvar ögonblicket då jag snorklade i lugnt klart hav och bottnen försvinner i blått – plötsligt flyger jag upp och ner; tittar upp och den silvriga ytan krusar sig som en bädd av moln, tittar ner och där finns inget annat än himlen.

Genom alla de grå månaderna rör jag vid min panna för att känna om jag ännu bär det där blå ögonblicket inom mig. Om våren medan heden dränerar ut sig genom kulvertar under mitt hus, utan yta, utan färg, sluter jag ögonen och lyssnar hur mina andetag raspar genom gummislangen, känner mina simtag bära mig framåt, andas, blått, andas, blått, andas, blått.

Kulvertarna rinner ner i floden, som flyter runt byn. I staden där jag har ett kontor brukar också floden, nergiftad och oljig, smyga sig bakvägar, men då ett hamnområde är en självskriven del av förnyelsekonceptet, äter jag nu min lunch bland lasthus som byggts om till kaféer, barer, lägenheter, ett shoppingcenter, en flerskärmsbiograf. Jag väntar mig att en båt eller en simmare skall störa den klara bruna ytan och undrar om någon, annat än metare eller måsar, skulle märka om vattnet byttes ut till glas.

Jag äter min sandwich, tittar upp på himlens alla korsvägar av flygstrimmor, ett skylandskap som du skulle ha lika svårt att känna igen som stadens utseende nu. När jag såg på himlen med dig skulle det ha tagit en hel dag att väva lika många strimmor, andas, blått, andas, blått, andas.

## 1  Colour

The winter hills behind my home sponge into bog. I hang on to that moment, snorkling in calm clear sea when the bottom disappears into blue – suddenly you're flying upside down: look up and the silver surface ripples away like a bed of cloud, look down and there's nothing but sky.

All through the grey months I touch my forehead to check I still carry that blue moment inside me. In spring while the moor drains through culverts under the house, without surface, without colour, I close my eyes and listen to my breath rasp through the rubber tube, feel my strokes carry me forward, breath, blue, breath, blue, breath, blue.

The culverts run into the river that flows round the village. In the city where I have an office, the river used to skulk in a poisonous slick round the back of things too, but waterfront is an essential part of the regeneration kit and I eat my lunch among warehouses converted to cafes, bars, apartments, shops, a multiplex. I wait for a boat or a swimmer to ply the bright brown surface and wonder, if the water were replaced with glass, whether anyone but anglers or gulls would notice.

I eat my sandwich, look up at the criss-cross of air-wakes, a skyscape that would be as unrecognisable to you as the way the city looks now. When I watched the sky with you it would take all day to weave as many vapour trails, breath, blue, breath, blue, breath.

*2   Yta*

Floden Aires klibbiga flöde får mig att tänka på den där gången i förra århundradet, då vi vandrade längs hamnen i Västervik, och du sa *titta därborta*. Alltid när du sa *titta därborta* med den där pressade, snabba tonen och fingrade på dina pärlor, såg jag alltid åt motsatt håll. Jag är inte säker på om jag såg pojkens kropp, eller bara de krökta ryggarna på de nyfikna, men jag har en bild av tanken, så dykarens mask upp ur vattnet, en hand på träbryggan, den andra som lyfter något vitt och slappt till ytan.

Nästa dag simmade jag ut till en vik med klippor och tallar, klättrade upp på en dykplattform och fastnade. Då jag såg ner i det grumliga gröna vattnet visste jag att det gråvita skimret i ändan av kättingen inte var en kropp, bara nedtyngda plastbehållare som höll flotten på plats, men jag kan ännu känna hur det vände sig i magen, hur kallt det varma vattnet var, som omklamrade bröst och nacke, då jag simmade tillbaka med hopknipna ögon, studsade upp på tårna så snart jag nuddade botten, sprang så fort jag kunde tvinga mina knän till.

Detta hände långt innan jag rörde vid en död kropp, din, fascinerad av hur du tycktes tömd på all fuktighet, fraktalmönstret över din hud som torkade lerytor.

## 2  *Surface*

The sticky flow of the Aire brings back that time in the last century, we were walking along the dock in Västervik, you said *look over there*. Whenever you said *look over there* in that scrunched, hurried tone, touching your pearls, I looked wherever you were pointing away from. I am not sure if I saw the boy's body, or just the rubberneckers lurch back, but I have an image of the tank then the mask of the diver surfacing, one hand on the wooden dock, the other bringing something white and floppy to the surface.

The next day I swam out into a pine and granite bay, climbed onto a diving platform and got stuck. Looking down into the cloudy green water I knew the grey white shimmers at the end of the chain were not a body, just weighted plastic containers anchoring the raft, but I can still feel the sick in my stomach, how cold the warm water was, clutching my chest and neck as I swam ashore, eyes closed tight, tip-toe bounced as soon as I touched bottom, ran as soon as I could force my knees.

This was long before I touched a body, yours, fascinated how you seemed drained of moisture, the fractal pattern of your skin like dry mud flats.

*3   Sjöben – min korta karriär i flottan*

Bortamatch någonstans ute på slättlandet, min debut under fjorton, Penninerna försvunna i dis, Wales berg knappt mer än ett rykte, bara flata fält efter flata fält, match efter match in i ett giftgult fjärran, små figurer som speglar i speglar. Du satt i bilen och lyssnade till radion medan Baker, vår halvback, gjorde tricket som fick tiden att stanna. Om jag varit uppe ur gruffet snabbt nog, hade jag sett honom ta emot och ge bollen rätt upp i ansiktet på sin förlamade motståndare. Allting stannade upp medan Baker vägde sina alternativ: sparka? tackla och springa? kasta ut i vid båge? Eller vända tiden tillbaka, mata in bollen på nytt, ha oss alla att falla över varann i en hög – som Keystone Cops – januariknepet för dumma forwardar, tackla, retirera, opp, bollen redan miltals borta, jaga, tackla, retirera, opp, bollen är redan … jaga, blått, andas, blått, andas, blått, andlös. Baker står där med bollen i händerna men helt olik sig, så vi ser alla åt samma håll som han …

Ett rödgult fartygsskrov rostfläckar, vit överbyggnad rostfläckar, en hög av containrar, ett helt kvarter lägenheter som rör sig ur dimman längs häcken bakom målstolparna, besättningen uppe på kommandobryggan, ser oss inte, radarrektangeln som snurrar, en svärm av måsar och kor i släpvattnet. Vi är alla på sju famnars vatten, till och med domarn, visslan i mun, armen utsträckt liksom bortglömd. Baker säger ingenting, hans läppar rör sig men han säger ingenting – sen sänder han i väg ett massivt skott som faller så snöpligt nära att vi inser att fartyget är mycket större än vi trodde. The Ship Canal är inte längre Geografi.

Jag följer fartyget. En vecka senare är vi i en u-båt, 57 kilometer inåt land från Irländska sjön, 100 kilometer från en navigerbar Humber, 18 meter över havet, Manchester hamn, öppet hus hos Royal Navy, köar för en titt i periskopet på folk som köar längs kajen för en titt i en u-båt.

## 3  Sea legs – my brief naval career

An away game out in the flatlands, my under-14 debut, the Pennines misted out, the Welsh mountains no more than a rumour, just flat field after flat field, game after game into the chemical distance, tiny figures like mirrors in mirrors. You sat in the car listening to the staticky radio while Baker, our fly half, did that thing that made time stand still. If I was up out of the scrum quick enough I'd see him receive and present the ball end up in his stalled opponent's face. Everything stopped while Baker weighed his options: Kick? Shimmy and run? Pass out wide? Or rewind time, feed the ball back in, have all of us falling in on top of ourselves – the Keystone Cop pack – the January slog for stupid flankers, maul, ruck, up, the ball already miles off, chase, maul, ruck, up, the ball already … chase, blue, breath, blue, breath, blue, breathless. Baker standing there, the ball in his hands but different from usual so we all look the way he's looking …

An orange hull and rust, white superstructure and rust, a stack of containers, a block of flats moving out of the mist along the hedge behind the goal posts, crew high on the bridge oblivious to us, the spinning radar, a wake of seagulls and cows. We're all at sea, even the ref, whistle in mouth, arm out forgotten. Baker says nothing, his lips move but he says nothing then launches a massive kick that falls so way short we realise the ship is even bigger than we thought. The Ship Canal no longer Geography.

I follow the ship. A week later we are in a submarine, 57 kilometres inland from the Irish Sea, 100 kilometres from navigable Humber, 18 metres above sea level, Manchester Docks, Royal Navy Open Day, queuing for a look through the periscope at people queuing on the quayside for a look in a submarine.

Några veckor senare gungar jag på en klibbig kanal, 152 meter över havet, 65 kilometer från Dees mynning, 42 kilometer från Nordsjön, en nybörjarsjöscout i Macclesfield församling, inte på en fartygskanal, definitivt inte en artär, knappt en ådra, en kanotkanal, ett smalt snöre att dra mig fram längs efter kungsfiskare och trollsländor.

När sommaren gått har jag lärt mig segla genom att kryssa mot fem slussportar, en bilparkering, pelargången till en herrgård, och jag deltar i en tävling på en reservoarsjö, 141 meter över havet, 3 meter från trädbankar, seglande en blixtjolle i bleke, jag sitter och ser hur ankor och hundägare passerar mig, båten blir så uttråkad så hon rycker ner sitt hisståg, och gaffeln ramlar ner tillräckligt nära örat för att jag ska fatta vinken, stiga ur och dra henne i land, en regatta utmarsch.

A few weeks after that I'm wobbling on a canal slick, 152 metres above sea level, 65 kilometres from the Dee Estuary, 42 kilometres from the North Sea, a 1st Congregational Macclesfield Sea Scout, not on a ship canal, certainly not an artery, hardly a vein, a canoe canal, a narrow thread to pull myself along after kingfishers and dragonflies.

By the summer I've learnt to sail by tacking towards five bar gates, a car park, the portico of a stately home, and I'm in competition on a reservoir, 141 metres above sea level, three metres from tree banks. Sailing a Mirror on a mirror, I sit watching ducks and dogwalkers overtake me, my boat gets so bored she snaps her own halyard, the gaff crashing down close enough to my ear for me to take the hint, so I step overboard and drag her ashore, a regatta walkout.

*4   Flak av land*

Trotsa den sista höjden innan du rullar nerför hemåt på Skipton-Ilkley vägen och där står de fyra vita vindturbinerna på Chelker reservoaren. 80 kilometer från Irländska sjön, 120 kilometer till östkusten, 221 meter över havet. Inte ett stort stycke vatten, kanske en kilometer långt, två hundra meter brett.

Här blåser ibland vinden från fyra håll samtidigt. Jag har plattats ut av vindstötar rätt ut från stallväggar, sett vatten spruta uppåt, hoppa som en fisk ur slät stiltje. Strömmar löper iväg och vänder tillbaka som om de glömt nånting – ytan sjunker in, virvlar, toppar sig, och lägger sig igen sekundsnabbt till ett fulländat molnlandskap.

Detta var den sista väg jag körde tillsammans med dig, jagande en blå och röd varmluftballong som hängde över den östra horisonten, glödande av solnedgången, den lyste i det mörka väderstrecket, vi lyste i accelererande silver längs den dubbla körbanans långa svep tillbaka hem till mig, mätta av en dag uppe vid floden Wharfes källor.

Varsomhelst i världen kan jag sluta ögonen och kliva bakåt över dalarna, se åt nordväst mot Great Close Scar. 465 meter över havet, 42 från Morcambe Sands, 128 från Flamborough Head, 90 meter ovanför Malham tjärn, ett stenkummel, snö, vi är tre som stretar uppför fårstigar genom frusna buskage för att låta dig flyga i vinden över smältvattnet ut i flödena på bergets båda sidor, land, torso, Great Close Scar.

Varje gång jag kör upp förbi Chelker, vilar en ångare på den mörka ytan, vita ljus hänger bogspröt – mast – skorsten – skorsten – mast – stäv, däcken varma, upplysta för drinkar, dans, pärlor, jollen du sänt för att hämta mig.

## 4  Land Floe

Breast the last hill before dropping down home on the Skipton-Ilkley road, and there are the four white wind turbines of Chelker Reservoir. 80 kilometres from the Irish Sea, 120 kilometres to the east coast, 221 metres above sea level. Not a big bit of water, maybe a kilometre long, two hundred metres wide.

Sometimes the wind blows four ways at once. I have been flattened by blasts straight out of barn walls, seen water spurt upwards, leap like a fish from flat calm. Currents make little runs before turning back as if they've forgotten something – the surface pits, whorls, ridges, and in an instant lies back, a perfect cloudscape.

This was the last road I drove with you, chasing a red and blue hot air balloon on the eastern horizon, blazed by sunset. Anywhere in the world I can close my eyes and step the valleys back, look north-west to Great Close Scar. 465 metres above sea level, 42 from Morecambe Sands, 128 from Flamborough Head, 90 metres above Malham Tarn, a cairn, snow, three of us scrabbling the sheep paths and frozen clumps to give you up into the wind onto the melt into the flow each side of the hill, country, torso, Great Close Scar.

Every time I come up past Chelker, a liner sits on the dark surface, white lights hung bowsprit – mast – funnel – funnel – mast – stern, decks warm, lit for drinks, dancing, pearls. You have sent the tender chugging shoreward to collect me.

5  *Snäcka*

                              penninskt tvärsnitt
                                      hed
                                                      skog
                                    ås
             mynning      slätt              dal              mynning


            Jag har nött fram min vardagsrutin i tågspår, på motorvägar, från kust till kust.


Jag kartlägger positioner och är omedelbart någon annanstans, havsnivå väst. Tänker på hem, Manchester. befinner mig på havsnivå väst: Mersey, Liverpool Passkontor, plockar upp den lilla svartblå boken mitt första ID som annat än /Child/Enfant/Barn Accompanied by/ Accompagne de/ I sällskap av men fortfarande mer Imperium än Europa, British subject/ Citizen of United Kingdom. Minns hur du körde, sökte utfarten ur staden, passerade en lång hamnmur av kranar och båtskorstenar, nästa dag: Immingham, havsnivå öst: flammor från raffinaderier, du viftar adjö till mig medan jag glider ut genom mynningen, till Rotterdam, Köpenhamn, Göteborg, Helsingfors, Leningrad, billig Dubonnet, Kazbek cigaretter. På tåget tillbaka, Moskva, Brest, Köln, Ostende kupéns britsar fulla av en familj som packar upp sig, korv, ost, vodka. Tredje morgonen, nästan hemma öppnar jag vagnsdörren åt det håll restaurangvagnen fanns kvällen innan – bara järnvägsräls som försvinner, stiger ut i ett snabbt intet, luft i knäna, knäar på vatten.

Tio år senare sände du adresserade färdigt frankerade kuvert, postkort med kryssrutor söderut,

Kommer du ☐
                              Hem i sommar
Kommer du inte ☐

Nu är jag tillbaka, jag försörjer mig på platser jag i många år passerade och tänkte tack gode gud att jag inte är född här: stads-skrov, bakbundna med insparkade tänder, puff

## 5  Helix

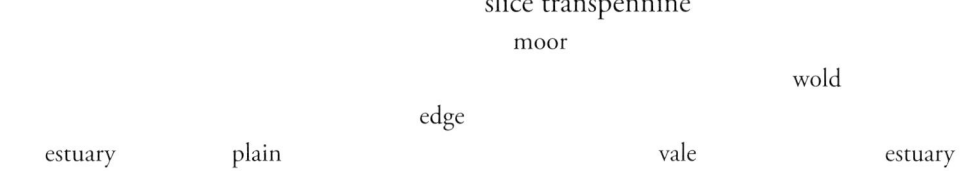

I've worn my groove in train tracks, motorways, coast to coast.

I plot a position and am immediately somewhere else. Thinking of home, Manchester, I am at sea level West: Merseyside, Liverpool Passport Office, picking up the little blue-black book my first ID not as a Child/Enfant Accompanied by/Accompagne de; but still more Empire than Europe, British Subject, Citizen of United Kingdom and Colonies. Thinking of you driving, trying to find the road out, skirting a long dock wall of masts and funnels, I am already in the next day: sea level East, Immingham: refinery flares, you waving as I slip the estuary, to Rotterdam, Copenhagen, Gothenburg, Helsinki, Leningrad, cheap Dubonnet, Kazbek cigarettes. On the train back, Moscow, Brest, Köln, Ostende, the compartment's bunk beds full of a family unwrapping themselves, sausage, cheese, vodka.

The third morning, nearly home I open the carriage end door to where the restaurant car had been the night before – nothing but track disappearing, stepping into fast nothing, air in the knees, kneeling on water.

Ten years later you were sending stamped addressed envelopes, postcards with tick boxes south,

Are You ☐
                         Coming Home This Summer
Are You Not ☐

Now I am back, my livelihood in places I passed for years thinking thank god I wasn't born there: skele-towns, their hands tied behind their backs, their teeth kicked in, boof

lågkonjunktur, puff dogmer, puff billigare arbetskraft utomlands. Stenlejon som strandat på döda fabriker. Platser jag lärt mig andas i, en krans av kranar, sandblästring, glasfönster som speglar himlen, nytt vatten, långsam inströmning av människor. Och över bergkammarna norrut, sluttande gröna betesmarker, torrstensmurar, en ångare på en liten brun sjö.

Då jag flyger in över Manchester eller Leeds Bradford, över endera kusten, plockar jag upp bandet av Humber eller Mersey. vägar, spår, Penninernas breda mörka flod korsad av nya flöden, West Yorkshire Greater Manchesters ljusträngsel, städer, förstäder, shopping, matställen, bowling, filmöar, plåtskjul, trafik från topp till tå, isgrönt upplysta pölar för hockey, five-aside. Ibland närmar man sig Ringvägen västerifrån, de sista finterna, svängar, skutt, öppna flappar och flygbromsar – där genom vingen Tattons smala sjö där jag lärde mig segla bland vass och kanadagäss – jag sträcker på armarna, håller andan, slår i vågen av asfalt, jämkar in på landningsbanan, en munfull hemkomst.

recession, boof dogma, boof cheaper labour elsewhere. Stone lions left stranded atop dead mills. Places I've learnt to breathe in, now a ribbon of cranes, sand-blasting, glass in the windows reflecting sky, new water, the slow influx of people. And stepping across ridges north, the slanted green of pasture, dry stone walls, the liner sat on the little brown lake.

Flying into Manchester or Leeds Bradford, crossing either coast, I pick up the ribbon of Humber or Mersey, roads, tracks, the wide dark river of the Pennines criss-crossed with new streams, the West Yorkshire Greater Manchester cram of lights, towns, out of towns, shopping, eating, bowling, film islands, tin warehouses, traffic nose-to-tail, bright flood green pools of hockey, five-aside. Sometimes approaching Ringway from the west, the last shimmies, sways, bobs, all open flaps and airbrakes – there through the wing, Tatton's thin lake where I learnt to sail among the reeds and Canada geese – I stretch my arms, hold my breath, hit the wave tarmac, settle into the runway, a mouthful of homecoming.

*6   Volym*

Högt uppe på fördäck på färjan Vancouver till Victoria längtar jag efter att valar skall uppenbara sig, vill se dem överallt, ingenstans, valtystnad, valvissling, valdjup, valar djupt därnere.

I sjätte klassen åkte jag med en vän på fiskelov till Irland. En dag hyrde vi en liten båt och rodde ett par sjömil ut på sjön. Mitt om eftermiddagen hör jag ett lätt drillande av fallande vatten, ett mjukt men annorlunda simtag, ser upp från mitt spö och ser Tim med frusen mun, stirra förbi mig, jag vänder mig om och knappt tjugo meter ifrån är en valstjärt på väg ut i havet. Vi sitter blickstilla, väntar på en val – tänker på storleken på valrevben och storleken på plankton, på vilken smäll en valstjärt kan utdela, hur båten skulle lyftas, splittras. Två roddtag från land en lång väg. Andas, andas, andas, andas, andas, blått, valen syker upp ungefär lika långt borta och blåser. Fradga. Lättnad. Åror. Strand. Resten av veckan fiskade vi i floder.

Högt uppe på fördäck på färjan Vancouver till Victoria repeterar jag historien om en val som dyker upp, en sprutning, en rullning, fallande tillbaka under ytan. Ingenting. Inga valar. Bara Mount Baker så långt borta i US of A.

De flesta resor jag gjorde som barn, Southampton till Cherbourg, Immingham till Göteborg eller Rotterdam, Helsingör till Hälsingborg var du nere i hytten feberögd av sjösjuka.

Du har sett så lite av mitt liv, men då jag ser Mount Baker inser jag hur mycket av mitt liv du fyller, vårt långdistansspråk, din närhet, som fyller ytan.

## 6  *Volume*

High on the foredeck of the Vancouver to Victoria ferry I long for whales to surface, see them everywhere, nowhere, whale silence, whale zilch, whale depth, whales down there.

In sixth form I went to Ireland with a friend on a fishing holiday. One day we hired a little boat and rowed a mile off shore. In the middle of the afternoon I hear a light trill of falling water, a soft but different lap, look up from my rod to see Tim mouth frozen, staring past me, I turn and not twenty yards away a whale tail slots itself into the sea. We sit waiting a while for a whale – think about the size of whale ribs and the size of plankton, the whack that whale tail could give, how the boat would lift, splinter. Two clicks off shore suddenly a long way out. Breath, breath, breath, breath, breath, breath, blue, the whale surfaces about the same distance further out and blows. Spume. Relief. Oars. Shore. The rest of the week we fished rivers.

High on the foredeck, Vancouver to Victoria, I rehearse the story of a whale breaking, a spout, a roll, falling back under. Nothing. No whales. Only Mount Baker so far off in the US of A.

Most voyages I made as a kid, Southampton to Cherbourg, Immingham to Gothenburg or Rotterdam, Helsingør to Helsingborg, you were down below bright eyed with sea sickness.

You have seen so little of my life, but seeing Mount Baker so big, so far off, I realise how much of my life you fill, our long distance language, your imminence, filling the surface.

*Carita on Kath*

When the English Interland team came to Finland in September 2004 we cruised around Ostrobothnia reading the first Interland texts. My first impression of Kath, from the first Litfest in 2001, was then confirmed: she was fast, energetic and straightforward in reading-performances as well as in discussions. A small miracle of speed.

We realised we had a lot in common. Both of us were among the first to go to university in our non-academic, large and loud families. And we both survived. During the stay in Finland she was the one who convinced me I should come over to Yorkshire together with the two other Finnish writers. I had hesitated due to my slight physical handicap. But Kath offered solutions: 'Just tell us what you need, Jacuzzi, reflexology treatments…whatever!' Who on earth could resist such kind offers!

Translating means diving deep into texts, trying to move around in their universe much like the writer would do. I have felt very much at home in Kath´s poetical universe. She translates very well into Swedish: her language, laconic, full of withheld emotion behind the apparent; her wry sense of humour; her sharp but understanding eye for people´s peculiar ways and sayings. Difficult experiences of loss and grief emerge as elusive tensions in the texts.

She's also been a conscientious close-reader of my texts, ever patient, suggesting alterations when my English tends to be too pompous for its own good. Our exchange here has been rewarding. You sense that Kath has a substantial knowledge of working with other people's texts, done in the most varying circumstances. In the midst of intense 'Interlanding' she was off for a ten day stay in Malawi guiding budding writers there into the craft of writing. That energy again.

The constant to-and-fro between the two languages has been most exciting: a bit like swimming side by side in a vast ocean of words. I'm reminded of the delicious changes between hot and ice-cold in the Turkish baths in Harrogate. An experience of awakening.

Does it have to have an ending, I ask myself, dreaming up ways of extending this project into further realms: Siberia maybe or – even better – White Sea Carelia, homeland of the Kalevala and the strange white whales.

# Aiming for Still Water

## Mot stilla vatten

### Kath McKay

*Who'll now lead us to water
go with us to the river?*
        *Kalevala: 24*


*Ken nyt vie ve'elle meitä,
Ken juoelle juohattavi?*
        *Kalevala: 24*

*Stella Maris*

Mariastoden sträcker sina armar över hamnen
där unga pojkar dyker i klart vatten
fläckat av dieseldroppar. Färjan skär igenom
The Narrows, släpper ner fronten när den närmar sig land.
Bilar startar. Två män i keps på Cuan Arms
pratar om Sean, som inte varit över
på tjugo år, men är nyss hemkommen.

Het whiskey glider lätt ner i november
när havstjockan rullar in och det långa tjutet
från livbåten bryter in i sömnen. Inspektörer
från England säger att båtfärgen är giftig
för fiskar. Svampgift sätter sig, djupt nere. Här i norr
är vi alltid utsatta för följder. Klara nätter
kan man se Vintergatan, och en galax av stjärnor;
Calisto och Cassiopeia. Hundstjärnan, Plogen

och vid St Brigids källa, trasor på hagtornsbuskar och alar
med nedskrivna önskningar. Kära Gud bota henne
Jesus uppfyll min önskan. I rösena döljer
stenar stalagmiter. Nitrater läcker in i
vattencisternen. Fossiler i sanden. På stranden
upprivna stenar, människor mumlar en bön
säger det gick fort på slutet för henne, tur nog.

*Stellar Maris*

Mary's statue reaches arms across the harbour
Where boys dive into clear water
flecked with diesel. The ferry cuts through
The Narrows, lets its front down as it nears shore.
Cars start up. Two men in caps at the Cuan Arms
discuss Sean, who hasn't been over
for twenty years, but is just after getting back.

Hot whiskey slides down easy in November
when the sea mist rolls in and the long call
of the lifeboat breaks into your sleep. Inspectors
from England say the boat paint is toxic
to fish. Fungicides root, bed deep. This north
we're not without consequence. On clear nights
the Milky Way is visible, and a galaxy of stars;
Calisto and Cassiopeia. The Dog Star. The Plough

and at St Brigit's Well, rags on a hawthorn bush, alders,
scribbled wishes. Please God cure her,
Jesus grant my plea. In the cairns, boulders
cover stalagmites. Nitrates leach into the water
table. Fossils on the beach. On the shore
uprooted stones, people mumbling a prayer
say he went quick at the end, how people ought to.

*Floden*

    'Och Walkers Crisps var allt för honom'

Uttala 'Walker' med enkla v. Kasta huvudet bakåt.
Be sonen berätta historien: 'Den kvällen drack vi många öl.
Vi gick och gick, så satte vi oss vid Themsen. Min far,
han har aldrig sett en flod som rinner en väg om morgonen.
En annan om kvällen. Min far, han blir förvånad över sånt.
Jag tror att allt i England blir väldigt virrigt för honom –
London, Walkers-kexen, de många ölen, floden
som om morgonen flyter en väg och om kvällen en annan.'

*The River*

> *'And Walkers Crisps meant everything to him'*

Pronounce 'Walker' with a 'v'. Throw back the head.
Have his son tell the story: 'That night we drank many beers.
We walked and walked, and sat by the Thames. My father,
he has never seen a river that in the morning flowed one way
and in the evening another. My father, he is amazed at such things.
I think everything in England is mixed up together for him –
London, the Walkers crisps, the many beers, the river
that in the morning flows one way and in the evening another.'

*Kanalpromenad*

Vi vandrar längs Prinsengracht, Amsterdam,
ett hotell flyter ett stycke längre bort, ut mot havet.

Min gummistövel sjunker in i leran och mamma ropar åt mig.

En lukt kommer från Krugfelder Pancake House
med dess 'Allt du kan äta' skyltar. Kaffehus. En doft av bränt.

Det är mellan sen eftermiddag och kväll.
Löv från alar faller ner i vattnet.
Vi har gjort rundturen på sex språk,

vet att kanalen är till två tredjedelar cyklar, en tredjedel lera
som Flann O´Briens två tredjedelar cykel, en tredjedel man,
foten i balans, övergår helt i cykel.

Jag kunde leva i denna stad, där kvinnor i aftonklänning åker cykel
och gamla män bär korgar på magen och vid sidorna.
Vi stannar en med vilda örsnibbar, frågar om vägen till Rembrandtarna;

allting är ljusbrunt och skuggor,
en ny doft av hav.

*Canal Walk*

We walk by the Prinsengracht, Amsterdam,
a hotel floats further off, out to sea.

My wellington boot's sinking into mud and my mother is shouting at me.

There's a scent from the Krugfelder Pancake House,
with its 'All you can eat' signs. Coffee houses. A burnt smell.

It's between late afternoon and evening.
Alder leaves drop into the water.
We've done the tour in six languages,

know the canal is two thirds bicycle, one third mud
like Flann O'Brien's two thirds bicycle, one third man,
foot poised, becoming all bicycle.

I could live in this city, where women in evening dress ride side-saddle
and old men carry baskets on the front and sides.
We stop one with wild earflaps, ask the way to the Rembrandts;

everything is brown light and shadows,
a new smell of the sea.

´Jag är från Oldham. Bott här i femti år`.

Mina gummistövlar har sugit fast, och mamma ropar åt mig.

Grävmaskinerna krafsar efter barnvagnar, cyklar, en död hund.
Lastpallar och en sängram vinschas upp.
Bevis för vattnets magi, det döljer allt.

Min gummistövel var grön och jag var stolt över den,
undvek senare pölar i vår nybyggda vägs sprickor.

Jobbarna skrattar när blad ur en bok fladdrar ut,
blir solkiga och oläsliga. Feta duvor sitter på en bro,
en kvinna samlar in sitt paraply. En butik
som säljer gökur av indiskt lövsågat trä.

Vi går över, redo att betrakta ansikten, skuggor och halvdagrar.
Redo att på nytt betrakta tingen.
Under vattnet. Andas in.

'I am from Oldham. Been here fifty years.'

My wellington boot's sucked in, my mother is shouting at me.

Dredgers squelch trolleys, bicycles and a dead dog.
Wooden pallets and a bed frame are winched up.
Testimony to the magic of water, which covers.

My wellington was green and I was proud of it;
afterwards avoided puddles in the cracks of our newly built road.

Workmen laugh as pages flutter from a book,
 become sodden, illegible. Fat pigeons squat on a bridge,
a woman reins in her umbrella. There's a shop
that sells cuckoo clocks out of Indian fretted wood.

We cross, ready to view faces, those shadows and half tints,
Ready again to look at things.
Underwater. Breathe in.

*Aska*

Efter att vi kastat min mors aska i Mersey
gick vi till toaletterna vid Pier Head för att tvätta händerna.
En vakt i ett fyrtitals förkläde, med lång pannlugg
och mörkt läppstift, som Baby Jane, sa 'Sorry, love,
vattnet är avstängt.' Abseilers klättrade på Royal Livers fasad
Vi sög i oss glasstrutar. Torkade händerna i Savett.
Slickade fingrarna.

*Ashes*

After we threw my mother's ashes into the Mersey
we went to the Pier Head toilets to wash our hands.
An attendant in a 1940s pinafore, with long bangs
and dark lipstick, like Baby Jane, said 'Sorry, love,
the water's off.' Abseilers scaled the Royal Liver buildings.
We sucked ice-creams. Rubbed hands with baby-wipes.
Licked our fingers.

*Snö i håret*

December. Vi går in på turistbyrån med snö i håret,
frågar efter simhallen. Prognosen lovar snöstorm.
Vi har suttit i en timme på buss 99. Åtminstone två mänskor
har en kärleksaffär. Vi ser passagerare i flera butiker.
Jag köper en svart boucle-jacka. På ett tehus kl. 4.30
finns inget annat att äta än tekakor.
Vi smuttar på Orange Pekoe. I simhallen kan Kate inte
hitta omklädningsrummet. Jag för henne till den grunda ändan.
Genom fönstren ser vi snö lysa upp fälten.


*Simtur*

I rum nummer 13 simmar vi på torra land.
I dag säger yogaläraren 'crawla' och vi sträcker ut armarna.
'Sitt på ändan' säger hon. 'Sträck på ryggraden.' 'Simma.'
Fönstren vätter mot bassängen, där tränarna ropar 'Andas.'
Jag hör simmare genom glaset.
Blås ut, andas in, blås ut, andas in.
Hjärtat slår långsammare. Dunk, vänd, plask.


*Simbassänger i Leeds*

Pudsey,
Bramley,
Wetherby,
Armley.

Scott Hall,
Morley,
Östra Leeds.

Chippendale,
Fearnville,
Kippax,
Kirkstall.

Holt Park,
Middleton,
Rothwell.

Aireborough,
Johna Smeaton,
Leeds

International,
Södra Leeds.

*Snow on our Hair*

December. We go in the tourist office with snow on our hair,
ask for the swimming pool. A blizzard is forecast.
We've spent an hour on the 99 bus. At least two people
are having an affair. We see passengers in several shops.
I buy a black bouclé jacket. In a teashop at 4.30
there is nothing to eat except teacakes.
We sip at Orange Pekoe. At the pool, Kate can't see
the changing room. I guide her to the shallow end.
Through the windows, snow lightens the fields.

*Swim*

In Activity Room 13, we are swimming on dry land.
Today the yoga teacher says 'crawl' and we reach with our arms.
'Sit on your bottoms' she says. 'Lengthen your spine.' 'Swim.'
Windows look out over the pool, where coaches shout 'Breathe.'
'Slow the breath' she says, and the air conditioning goes off.
I hear swimmers through glass.
Blow out, breathe in, blow out, breathe in.
The heart slows. Thump, turn, splash.

*Swimming Pools of Leeds*

Pudsey,
Bramley,
Wetherby,
Armley,

Scott Hall,
Morley,
East Leeds.

Chippendale,
Fearnville,
Kippax,
Kirkstall.

Holt Park,
Middleton,
Rothwell.

Aireborough,
John Smeaton,
Leeds

International,
South Leeds.

*En kropp*

Sylvia berättar att i Baptistkyrkan i Headingly
går de in för total nedsänkning. Inte det där
med att väta huvudet med några droppar vatten
nej, kroppen böjs framöver, människan skuffas
ner i dopkaret: ett, två, tre och
kyrkan, fylld av tjugo-trettiåringar med mobiltelefoner,
håller andan. Ett, två, tre och människan dyker upp
med ansiktet strömmande och prästen tänder ett ljus
bakom de nydöpta. Ansiktena glänser.
Han öppnar händerna: 'Jag är uppståndelsen och livet.'
Leder ut den häpna församlingen för att se chionodoxa.
Vårstjärnor i snön.

*One Body*

Sylvia tells me that in Headingley Baptist Church
they go in for total immersion. None of this
wetting of the head and a few drips of water
but bending the body over, pushing the person
into the baptistery: one, two, three
and the church, full of twenty and thirty year olds with mobiles,
holds its breath. One, two, three and the person surfaces,
face streaming and the minister sets a light
behind the newly baptized. Their face glows.
Opens his hands: 'I am the resurrection and the light.'
Leads the stunned congregation out to see chionodoxa.
The glory-of–the–snow.

*…lahet kylmi, lammet kylmi*
*Meren rannat rapsutteli*
*Kalevala: 30*

## Det jag minns

är hur platt din kropp var. Inga muskler,
                        ingen andning.
Ögonen slutna, ansiktet besviket.
Jag låg ovanpå dig, på vår svarta soffa;

samma plats där jag grät
fjorton år tidigare
när vi flyttade in det här huset.

I kistan är du ännu stelare.
Skärsår runt halsen, din mun förvriden.
Vår dotter rusar ut ur rummet.


I yoga ser jag en damm, grön och skum,
där du simmar;
Men det jag minns är mitt första pris,

oss på en nyårsfest. Storgrinande
berättar du för alla. En dement kvinna frågar mig
om och om igen 'Och vad är det du gör?'

## Jag simmar

Jag simmar i din barndoms vatten.
Varje morgon vid Manly, när de vitklädda
åldringarna lämnar hamnpoolen. Folk joggar,
                   vädrar hundar;
du är här i den fasta blicken i Pab´s ögon,
Michaels lätta stamning. I sättet de säger 'swimmers'
för tajta simbyxor, 'kostymer' i pluralis,
hur de insisterar att juicen är måltidens bästa del,
hur samtalet kommer in på kompost.
                        Blå västar på färjan,
det där aussie 'OK'. Jag simmar på hamnsidan,
du skulle vara i svallet. Varje morgon vaknar
                 jag före vår dotter,
simmar i din barndoms vatten. Lär mig på nytt.

*…chilled bays, chilled pools
struck seashores rigid*
$\qquad\qquad\qquad$ *Kalevala: 30*

## What I remember

is the flat of your body. No muscles, no breath.
Your eyes closed, face disappointed.
I lay on top of you, on our black sofa;

the same place I'd cried
fourteen years before
when we entered this house.

In the coffin, you are stiffer.
Cuts round your neck, mouth twisted.
Our daughter runs from the room.


In yoga I see a pond, green and murky,
you swimming;
But what I remember is my first award,

us at a New Year's Eve party. You grinning,
telling everyone. A woman with dementia asks me
again and again 'And what is it you do?'

## I am swimming

I am swimming in the waters of your childhood.
Every morning at Manly, after the white robed elders
leave the harbour pool. People jog, walk dogs;
you're here in that fixed look in Pab's eye,
Michael's slight stammer. In how they say 'swimmers'
for trunks; 'costumes' in the plural,
their insistence on 'juices' as the best part of a meal,
how talk turns to compost. Blue vests on the ferry,
that Aussie 'OK'. I'm swimming on the harbour-side,
you'd be in surf. Every morning I wake before our daughter,
swim in the waters of your childhood. Re-learn.

*Dina bröder ger dig tillbaka åt mig i Sydney*

I en ask med oranga blommor: dina brev från England,.
Annapurna, Istanbul, Kabul.

1974 och du har grävt ner dig i Camden. 'Jag klarar inte
en vinter till här.' Nästa vinter bäddar vi ner oss i Hackney.
Du skriver till Oz 'Den svåra delen av dagen är över.'
Barnen sover. Astma, underligheter och skola.

Vänner för din aska i en racerbåt till Pittwater,
Tio i en fem personers båt, fem ligger på bottnen, jagade
av kustbevakningen. Michael, barfota, med långt
grått hår, talar om slutet på din fysiska kropp.

Kate ser en stråle ljus 'exakt på det ställe' där askan sänks.
På land klagar Tony 'För mycket förbannad aska,
Pittwater fylls banne mig opp med aska.'
Jag letar i asken.
Första nattvarden, dopet, musikbetygen vid åtta år.

'Förbluffande hur mycket Phillip gått
framåt med så lite arbete.' Bilder av dig roende, i shorts,
du poserar i valprund pubertet innan du växer, tunnas ut.

Utsatt i kretslopp.

*Your brothers give you back to me in Sydney*

in an orange flowered box: your letters from England,
Annapurna, Istanbul, Kabul.

1974 and you're holed up in Camden. 'I can't imagine
another winter here.' Next autumn we bed down in Hackney.
You write to Oz 'The difficult part of the day is over',
children asleep. Asthma, quirks and school.

Friends take your ashes on a speedboat at Pittwater.
Ten in a five person boat, so five lie down, pursued
by Water Police. Michael, barefoot, with long
grey hair, speaks of the end of your physical body.

Kate sees a beam of light 'at the exact spot' the ashes tip in.
On shore, Tony complains 'Too many bloody ashes,
Pittwater's filling up with bloody ashes.'
I sift through the box.
Your first Communion, baptism, music report aged eight.

'Surprising how much progress Phillip has made
On so little work.' Pictures of you rowing, in shorts,
posing in puppy fat adolescence before you lengthen and thin.

Put into orbit.

*Lyöte lykkyvaattehisin,
Antipaitoihin paneite*
	*Kalevala: 14*

## Haj Känguru Krokodil

*Etikett för öar*
Gå inte i vattnet vid gryning eller skymning
Hajarna. Om natten krokodiler.
Rör alltid om vattenytan när du ska simma,
*Det är inte krokodilerna du ser som är problemet.*

Om fenor cirklar är hajar på hugget.
Bär alltid handskar när du jobbar i trädgården.
Giftspindelnät. Se upp med högt gräs. Dvärgpyton.
Sök genom sängen varje kväll efter ormar och ödlor.

Dra historier. ´Den var så här stor. ´Hon sköt den´.
´Han var rasande som en skuren orm.´ Uppskatta fem-före-situationer.
att nästa steg inte var ödesdigert. Frossa i drama, intriger,
repliker från dina favoritfilmer.


## Fiskar du inte såg

Coral trout (Chinese footballer trout) Plectropomus laevis Barramundi cod Cromileptes altivelis Striped marlin (Spearfish) Tetrapturus audax Wrasse (Goldspot Pigfish) Bodianus perditio Sawshark (Flake) Pristiophorus cirratus Barramundi Lates calcarifer Hapaka (Groper) Polyprion oxygeneios Blue-spotted coral cod Cephalopholis cyanostigma

*Elk Horse Swan*
      *Kalevala: 14*

## Shark Kangaroo Crocodile

*Island Etiquette*
Do not go into the water at dusk and dawn;
The sharks. At night it's crocs.
Always skim the water when swimming;
*It's not the crocs you can see should bother you.*

If fins circle, sharks will attack.
Always wear gloves when working in the garden.
Funnel webs. Be careful of long grass. Children's pythons.
Check your bed each night for snakes and lizards.

Tell stories: 'It was as big as this.' 'She shot him.'
'He was as mad as a cut snake.' Be thankful for near-misses,
that the next step was not fatal. Relish drama, plot,
the lines from your favourite movies.

## Fish You Did Not See

Coral trout (Chinese footballer trout) Plectropomus laevis Barramundi cod Cromileptes altivelis Striped marlin (Spearfish) Tetrapturus audax Wrasse (Goldspot Pigfish) Bodianus perditio Sawshark (Flake) Pristiophorus cirratus Barramundi Lates calcarifer Hapaka (Groper) Polyprion oxygeneios Blue-spotted coral cod Cephalopholis cyanostigma

*Olen maalla vierahalla,*
*Tuiki tuntemattomalla*
　　　*Kalevala: 7*

## *Fjorton veckor*

Min hud är knottrig av moskitbett.
Myror kryper över kremerad aska
I går natt vällde en tre fjärdedels måne

upp över öns andra sida.
Vi undviker att gå nära vattnet.
Historier här handlar om krokodiler,
　　　　　　　　eller närapå-olyckor

med en taipan, ett giftspindelnät eller en haj.
Jag har burit din aska
i en brun godisburk.

Fiona, en aborigin, tittar förbi med en båtlast
räkfiskare, för en öl och en cigarett.
Berättar att hon ska gifta sig med en,
　　　　　　　　och om pytonormen

som vecklat sig runt hennes baby.
'Du får ta den i huvet, veckla upp den.'
Vi skruvar av locket, strör ut dig från The Spit,

slungar ut dig i farleden vid Torres Strait,
dricker champagne. Fionas man är fyrti.
Hans hud är hundra år gammal.

## *Namn/ord*

Lämnar Kirribilli, Palm Beach, Avalon, Parramatta,
Först åker vi norrut in i ölstopens land.
Schooner. Pot, Tinny. Blowy.
Sen åker vi västerut till guld och bauxit landet.
Pinjarra. Wannanup. Dwellingup.
Utplånar snårskogen. Salt äter upp marken.
Nya namn. Port Bouvard. Lakeland. Paradise.

> *Yes, I am in a strange land*
> *utterly unknown*
>    *Kalevala: 7*

## Fourteen weeks

My skin is lumpy with mosquito bites.
Ants crawl over cremated remains.
Last night a three quarter moon welled up

over the other side of the island.
We don't walk too close to the water.
Every other story is a croc or a near miss

with a taipan, funnel web, shark.
I've carried your ashes
in a brown plastic sweet jar.

Fiona, an aborigine, stops off with a boatload
of prawn fishermen, for a beer and a smoke.
Says she's marrying one. And of the carpet snake

that wrapped itself round her baby?
'You take its head, unwrap.'
We unscrew the top, sprinkle you from The Spit,

swirl you into Torres Strait shipping lanes,
sip at champagne. Fiona's man is forty.
His skin is a hundred years old.

## Names/words

Away from Kirribilli, Palm Beach, Avalon, Paramatta,
First we go north into pin of beer country.
Schooner. Pot. Tinny. Blowy.
Then we go west to the land of gold and bauxite.
Pinjarra, Wannanup, Dwellingup.
Erasing the scrub. Salt eating the land
New names. Port Bouvard. Lakeland. Paradise.

*Stinger*

Efter medusan säger Maureen 'Ner i vattnet igen
och simma på. Som när du cyklar.'
Det efter att ha ringt till akuten i Perth,
där de säger 'Vinäger. Hur känner du dig
inombords?'
Det efter att ryggen börjat hetta och svällt upp,
ett rött pulserande sår.
Nästa morron stiger jag ner i klart vatten.
Fiskar kittlar mina fötter.

*Märken av Australien*

Medusans bett på ryggen.
Bett av moskiter och sandflugor på
benen.
Mina barn.

*En tieä …*
*Miten olla, kuin eleä;*
*Istun yön eli makoan,*
*Äijä on yötä*
          *Kalevala: 37*

*Niin ukko kipuja kiisti,*
*Työnti tuosta tuskanpäitä*
*Keskelle Kipumäkeä*
          *Kalevala: 9*

*After the Stinger*

After the stinger, Maureen says 'Get back
In the water and swim. Like riding a bike.'
This after phoning the emergency department in Perth,
them saying 'Vinegar. How do you feel in yourself?'
This after heat and swelling on my back,
a red pulsing wound.
Next morning I step into clear water
Fish tickle my feet.

*Australia marks*

The jellyfish sting on my back
The mosquito and sand fly bites on
my legs.
My children.

*I … do not know*
*how to be, which way to live.*
*I sit all night or I lie*
*There's much night*
     *Kalevala: 37*

*So the old man drove the aches*
*thrust them from the points of pain*
*to the middle of Ache Hill.*
     *Kalevala: 9*

*Till Phil som har blivit ett träd*

Jag ger dig mina frön Silvanus.
Mina spädbarn.
blåklinten från min trädgård,
aklejan och vallmon,
dammet i min Hoover,
husets handlingar Silvanus,
kontoutdragen,
röran under sängen,
mynten i soffan,
fruktsalladen som blandade sig på hemväg från
       affären.
Mina ägg mina varma bruna ägg.
Mina kyssar.

Fastän jag står i kanten av din äng
kommer jag inte över den.
Wetherby, Thursby, Earlby, Naseby.
Där finns björkar som blommar.
Deras bark vitnar, Betula papyrifera.
       Pappersbjörken.
Uramerikaner paddlar över floder, faller över
       kanten till Kanada.

Jag ger dig mina böcker Silvanus.
Träet till bordet vi gjorde av askträdet vi fällde.
Mitt skrivande, spindelord rafsade över handflatsstora
häften.
Mina händer Silvanus.
Mina ben.
Mina muskler.
Mina ögon.
Jag kan inte släpa på i denna sörja för evigt Silvanus.
Ogräs måste rensas ut, frön måste sås.
Jag vill ligga i min säng, begrava mitt huvud.
Men se på klockan. Mina fötter börjar röra sig igen.
En underjordisk ström rinner upp.
Du skall ge mig din välsignelse.

*To Phil who has turned into a tree*

I give you my seeds Silvanus
My babies
The cornflowers from my garden,
The aquilageia, the poppies,
The dust from my hoover,
The deeds to my house Silvanus,
The bank statements,
The mess from under the bed,
The coins from the sofa
The fruit salad that made itself on the way back
    from the market
My eggs my warm brown eggs
My kisses.

Though I stand at the edge of your field
I will not cross.
Wetherby, Thursby, Earlby, Naseby.
There are birch trees in blossom.
Their barks are whitening. Betula papyrifera.
    The paper birch tree.
Native Americans paddle over rivers, fall off the
    edge of Canada.

I give you my books Silvanus
The wood for the table we cut down from the ash tree.
My writing, spidery words scrawled across notebooks
the size of my palm
My hand Silvanus.
My legs.
My muscles.
My eyes.
I cannot squelch in this mud forever Silvanus.
There are weeds that need pulling, seeds sowing.
I would like to lie in my bed and bury my head.
But look at the clock. My feet will get moving again.
An underground stream will flow.
You will give me your blessing.

*Färger i Finland*

I Finland denna höst såg jag färg.
Tröjor i klara färger. Fläderbär. Blåbär.
Saft. Svampar. Tidigare, allt genom ett filter. Nu färg.


*Helsingfors*

I simhallen på Georgsgatan
är de flesta kvinnor nakna. Inte jag. De ler
när vi stöter till varandra, med mjuka delar av kroppen.


*Ordination*

Gör flera längder.
Simma i lätt crawl.
Andas regelbundet.
Drick mängder av vatten.
Upprepa.


*Att pejla*

Doppa i tån.
Så kroppen.
Skärpning. Lyssna, ett avlägset sus.
Ett fartyg för ankar.
Väj runt.
Pejla.

*Colours in Finland*

In Finland this autumn I saw colour.
The brightness of jumpers. Elderberry. Whortleberry.
Juice. Fungi. Before, everything through a filter. Now colour.


*Helsinki*

In the Yrjönkatu Swimming Hall,
most women naked. I'm not. They smile
as we bump, press soft bits of body.


*Prescription*

Take several lengths
Swim in an easy crawl
Breathe regularly.
Drink lots of water.
Repeat.

*Take Soundings*

Put your toe in.
Now your body.
Keen. Listen for a distant rush,
the kedge of a ship.
Circle round.
Sound.

*Steve on Ralf*

Driving Adam and me back late from Kokkola to Vaasa, Ralf pointed right and said, 'That's the farm where I was born, my family home.' We looked into the pitch blackness that we knew was yet more forest. Maybe we caught a glimpse of a track. I think I'm imagining there was a single light way down it.

I have a photograph of Ralf confronting a bear in York. We were with Marko and his partner Tiina, doing the tourist trail, and, in one of the serendipities that seem to run through this project, came across an exhibition of Baltic photographers in Impressions gallery. I took a photograph of Ralf in front of a photograph, Ralf staring at a bear on its hind legs, the bear staring at Ralf.

To those not knowing Swedish, most of Ralf's writing is hidden deep in the forest the bear will return to once Ralf has out-stared him. I catch glimpses – two poems in *Books from Finland*, six or seven translated for the Interland readings. Meantime, Ralf walked into two of my stories – as a driver on a long journey, and as a man with a doppelganger in his home town. Both were true stories published as fiction, and I realise now that in both I was exploring how male friendship deepens, and this friendship in particular.

Ralf is made up of polar contrasts. Intensely private, he is committed to the role of the writer animateur. His depth of reading, particularly in Anglo-Saxon writers, is matched by a passion for the demotic, the trivial, for retro-consumerism. He can talk to you about Bakelite. He'll drag you into the naff key-ring and flags of the union tourist tat shops. Ralf is a lively sedent, quiet for a winter, he'll suddenly hop on his bike and cycle the hundred kilometres to the family farm.

Ralf was the last of the six of us to bring his work to the table, and it came most complete. Maybe reading 'Yorkshire is covered with water' you'll sense the eclecticism of his influences – writers, music, films, or you'll catch a glimpse of his mania for collecting, hear the way he binds every greeting with the weather. The first of his poems I ever read is called 'Caesura' and the caesura is his natural space, observing in the lull, picking at the ineffable shape behind things, recording the atmosphere, fixing moments of movement conversation:

'…small demarcations
and corrections, openings
and dead ends, pauses
while we suck on mild cigarettes
and let the evening sink in without
feeling compelled to invent
anything to say. Soon enough
words arrive, and when they do
we know they are precisely ours and precisely the words
we have always been waiting for.'

# Yorkshire is covered with water

# Yorkshire är täckt av vatten

## Ralf Andtbacka

*Row thy boat down the sinews,*
  *Shake it down the limbs,*
*Row through gaps in bone,*
  *And through cracks in limbs.*
        *Kalevala: XV*

*Hammer [Groucho]: It's deep water, that's why a duck. It's deep water.*
        *The Cocoanuts, 1929*

  *Ro i ådrorna din eka,*
    *lägg i lemmarna din färdväg,*
   *ro i benens håligheter,*
    *leta dig längs dolda leder.*
        *Kalevala: XV*

I

Snöslask.

Joggade runt Metviken.
Nära dieselmotorfabriken kom de:
två fyllon vacklade ut,
sneddade över vägen,
fick plötsligt ett anfall
av raseri:

*satans hund satan din satans satans hund*

När man rör sig genom snöfall
i en blöt insvepande
smet av snö
. . .

klistersnö
man får in den
i bostaden hur man än försöker
torka av de där
skorna    mattorna blir
vattnade som hästar

(Borden här är uppochnedvända hovar
på förstörda ryttarstatyer)

II

*Vad är det du vill? Fortsätta andas?*
. . .

Alltid en massa snack
om berättelser   *Berättelser.*
men livet är

ett annat flöde.

Samma gamla heraklitiska,
alltid nytt.

Vad var det Marcus Aurelius skrev om
                            Herakleitos?

*Herakleitos berättade ofta för oss att världen skulle gå under genom eld. Men det var fukten som tog honom; han dog nersmetad med koskit.*

Du ska få en berättelse.

## I

Sleety snow.

I was jogging round Metviken.
Near the diesel engine factory they came:
two drunks staggering,
slanting across the road,
suddenly overcome
with rage:

*fucking dog fuck you fucking fucking dog*

When moving through falling snow
in a wet wrapping
sludge of snow
. . .

sticky snow
You get it inside
the house no matter how you
try to wipe those
shoes    the rugs get like
watered horses

(The tables here are the upturned hooves
of ruined equestrian statues)

## II

*What do you want? To go on breathing?*
. . .

Always a lot of talk
about stories    *Stories.*
but life is

a different flow.

The old Heraclitean one,
the same but always new.

What was it Marcus Aurelius wrote about
                                        Heraclitus?

*Heraclitus often told us the world would end in fire.*
*But it was moisture that carried him off; he died*
*smeared with cowshit.*

I'll give you a story.

*III*

1979 dog vår sista häst, en gammal hingst.
Strax före jul föll den ihop i sitt bås och min
far ringde efter nödslakten. Två män anlände.
Vi lyckades få ut hästen på stallgolvet, där den
ene av dem stack den i hjärtat. Men de ville
inte ha kadavret. Kanske var det så att min far
redan stuckit hästen – jag minns inte riktigt.
Men jag minns att den släpades ut och tömdes
på ångande inälvor. Men sen sa de att de inte
tänkte ta den. I nästan två veckor låg den på
rygg i snön med urgröpt buk och inälvorna
i en frusen hög vid sidan om. Dess ben och
hovar statylikt resta, i tjugogradig kyla.

*IV*

*Alkemistisk skrift*

(Låt det fasta förenas med
det flyktiga)

När ett fast ämne övergår till vätska,
kallas det smältning
När en vätska övergår till gasform,
kallas det ångbildning
När en gas övergår till vätska,
kallas det kondensering
När en vätska övergår till fast form,
kallas det stelning

(Fortsätt så processen
tills materian fått

den djupaste svarta färg)

## III

In 1979 our last horse died, an old stallion. Some time before Christmas it collapsed in the stall, and my dad phoned for emergency slaughter. Two men arrived. We managed to get the horse out on the concrete floor where one of them stabbed it in the heart. But they didn't want the carcass. Maybe Dad had already knifed the horse – I can't remember. But I do remember it being dragged outside and emptied of steaming entrails. And then they said they wouldn't take it. For almost two weeks it lay on its back in the snow, belly scooped out, intestines in a solid heap on the side. Its legs and hooves statuesquely raised, in twenty degrees of frost.

## IV

*Writing alchemy*

(Make the fixed volatile
and the volatile fixed)

When solid matter changes into liquid,
it is called melting
When liquid changes into gas,
it is called vaporisation
When gas changes into liquid,
it is called condensation
When liquid changes into solid matter,
it is called freezing

(Then continue the process
until the substance attains

the deepest shade of black)

V

Nyckelorden är:
*ansikte kropp händer hud*

Vattenskalle.

Platser:
*sjöar strömmar stränder cisterner badkar duschar*

Isballonger.
. . .

(Det regnar också på Titan,
men det är ett regn av flytande
metan, 180 grader kallt.)


VI

Yorkshire är täckt av vatten
och Whernside är en ö.

*Torrläggningsprojektet
var Nordeuropas största.*

VII

På hemväg från Kristinestad började
               det regna på allvar,
ett regn som blötte upp terrängen, tömde den på kallprat.

Jag vid ratten, Adam bredvid; Kath och Steve i baksätet.
Carita hade åkt till Korsnäs med egen bil.

I Långåminne vek jag av och vi åkte genom Malax,
sen vidare mot Sundom.

Vid Söderfjärden öppnade sig landskapet
*och vi svepte ner från heden och in i dalen.*

(Söderfjärden uppkom vid ett meteoritnedslag
för 520 miljoner år sedan.)
. . .

*Vi är på väg till Scarborough i morgon.
Det är alltid stormigt där den här tiden:
trottoarer sköljs ner i havet,
hotell störtar nerför branten.*

*V*

The key words are:
*face body hands skin*

Hydrocephalus.

Places:
*lakes streams shores cisterns showers tubs*

Ice balloons.
. . .

(There is rain on Titan too,
but it is a rain of liquid methane,
at minus 180 degrees.)


*VI*

Yorkshire is covered with water
and Whernside is an island.

*The drainage project was the
largest in Northern Europe.*

*VII*

On our return from Kristinestad,
                the rain grew more intense,
soaking the terrain, emptying it of small talk.

I at the wheel with Adam; Kath and Steve in the back.
Carita had gone to Korsnäs in her own car.

At Långåminne I turned left, and we passed through Malax
while heading for Sundom.

At Söderfjärden, the landscape opened up
*and we swept down from the moor and into the dale.*

(The Söderfjärden plain is the result of a meteorite impact
520 million years ago.)
. . .

*We're off to Scarborough tomorrow.*
*It's always stormy there at this time:*
*pavements washed into the sea,*
*hotels tumbling down the cliff.*

## VIII

Vad är det du vill? Fortsätta andas?
. . .
Den gången kunde jag inte simma,
var fem eller sex. Jag kom ut ur bastun
och vadade ut i sjön tills jag plötsligt
klev ner i intet.     Jag sjönk
under ytan men kom upp igen,
med vatten i näsa, hals, mun.
Upp/ner, upp/ner.

Senast jag hade samma känsla
var för en vecka sen, då min
badmintonkompis nämnde att
en bekants bekant kört genom isen
med snöskoter. När de hittade honom
på botten, satt han ännu kvar
med ett fast grepp om styret.
. . .
(Gör din egen undervattensmusik.
Spela dina egna melodier.
Välj dina egna instrument.
Mixa ditt eget ljud.
Spela sedan in dina kompositioner
med en orkester av undervattensväsen
och en kör av sjungande fiskar.)
. . .

## IX

*lort*

(fisk-, ko-, häst-)

## X

L är vattnets ljud
(lipa, lapa, läppja,
la la, lalla, lort)

Logr är vattnets runa
med allt vad det innebär:
tvätt, förändring, förlust

Germanska: *Laguz*
Gotiska: *Lagus*
Fornengelska: *Lagu*
Fornnordiska: *Logr*

Logr-runan är kopplad till
månen, natt och sömn.
(Fonetiskt värde: *l*)

## VIII

What do you want? To go on breathing?
. . .
That time I couldn't swim. I was
five or six. I came out of the sauna
and waded out in the lake,
where I suddenly stepped
into nothing.   I sank under,
resurfaced, water in nose, throat,
mouth. Up/down, up/down.

Last time I had that feeling
was about a week ago, when one of
my badminton buddies mentioned
that a friend of a friend drove his snowmobile
through the ice a few years back.
They found him down on the bottom,
still firmly gripping the handles.
. . .
(Make your own underwater music.
Play your own melodies.
Choose your own instruments.
Mix your own sound.
Then record all your compositions
with an orchestra of aquatic creatures
and a choir of singing fish.)
. . .

## IX

*shit*

(fish-, cow-, horse-)

## X

L is the sound of water
(lap, leak, liquid,
la la, lull, latrine).

Logr is the rune of water
and everything it implies:
washing, change, loss

Germanic: *Laguz*
Gothic: *Lagus*
Old English: *Lagu*
Old Norse: *Logr*

The logr-rune is associated with
the Moon, night and sleep.
(Phonetic value: *l*)

XI

Inlandsisen skrapade loss
och släpade med sig

lera, sand, grus, stenar och block.

(Gör en egen inlandsis.)

XII

*Istäcket, som var tre kilometer som tjockast,
pressade ner jordskorpan 800 – 1000 meter.
Ännu idag höjer den sig för att nå sitt forna
läge. I Kvarken är landhöjningshastigheten nu
8 millimeter/år. Geologer tror att landet ännu
kommer att stiga 100 – 125 meter.*

XIII

Strandfynd vid Mare Frigoris (flaskpost)
– daterat 11.4.2004

*Sent i går kväll stod jag och min far vid lidret
och lastade in lite ved i bilen. Ute på fältet
brann påskbrasan ännu, matad med plast.*

*När jag tittade upp såg jag hur klar himlen var
jämfört med i Vasa, en blåsvart duk
perforerad av droppande ljus.*

*Vägen hem var en sugande tunnel.
Hjulen rörde aldrig vid asfalten.
Landskapet kröktes, stjärnorna åldrades.*

*I baksätet vedsäckarna som bredaxlade,
tigande passagerare, deras löfte
om trygghet, värme, civiliserad eld.*

*XI*

The glacial ice scraped loose
and dragged along

clay, sand, gravel, rocks and boulders.

(Make your own glacial ice.)


*XII*

*The ice sheet, with a thickness of up to three
kilometres, pressed down the earth's crust 800
– 1000 metres. Today it is still rising to regain
its former level. In the Kvarken area, the rate of
uplift is now 8 millimetres a year. Geologists say
that the land will rise another 100 – 125 metres.*

*XIII*

Flotsam on the shore of Mare Frigoris (message in a
bottle) – dated 11/4/04

*Late last night I was out by the shed with my father
loading some firewood into the car. Out in the field,
the Easter bonfire was still burning, fed with plastic.*

*When I looked up, I noticed how clear the sky was
compared to Vasa, a darkly bluish cloth
perforated with dripping light.*

*The way home was a vacuum tunnel.
The tyres never touched the asphalt.
The landscape bent, the stars grew older.*

*In the backseat, the sacks of firewood
like broad-shouldered, silent passengers,
their promise of safety, warmth, civilising fire.*

*XIV*

(Ljussvärta, bländljus, nova)

Soligt i dag, men kallt.
Vi gick ut på isen,
rundade hamnbassängen
och tog sikte på Gustavsborg.
Ljuset från snön
fick ögonen att värka.
Vi stannade några gånger,
kisade mot horisonten
och fortsatte sen.
Under våra fötter –
högst sannolikt –

tröga små fiskar.

(Köldens hav)
. . .

Efteråt köpte jag en
guldpläterad sovjetisk
tändsticksaskhållare
med rymdmotiv för en euro
i en antikvitetsaffär
på Handelsesplanaden.

*XV*

Ångornas hav
Molnens hav
Regnets hav
. . .

(Kanalerna på Mars)

*XIV*

(Black blaze, blaze blind, nova)

Sunny but cold today.
We walked out on the ice,
rounding the basin and
making for Gustavsborg.
The light from the snow
made our eyes ache.
We stopped a few times
squinting at the horizon
before moving on.
Under our feet –
most likely –

sluggish little fish.

(Sea of Cold)

. . .

Afterwards, at an antique shop
in Handelsesplanaden,
I bought a gold-plated
Soviet matchbox holder
with a space age motif
for one euro.

*XV*

Sea of Vapour
Sea of Clouds
Sea of Rain

. . .

(The channels of Mars)

*XVI*

Ännu ett av dessa fragment
som flyter omkring: en
sommardag några år efter
att Neil Armstrong gjort
det första fotavtrycket
nära den sydvästra stranden
av Lugnets hav, såg jag min
morbror, maskinmästaren,
parkera sin bronsfärgade
Opel Manta på gården, stiga ut
och komma gående mot oss
där vi stod i garageporten.
Ett varggrin lyste i ansiktet.
Pilotglasögon, bullrande
       baryton.
. . .

(Det tar tio miljoner år
för det ständiga regnet
av mikrometeoriter
att röra om den översta
centimetern av månstoft.
Därför lär fotavtrycket
finnas kvar i minst
en miljon år, kanske två.)

*XVII*

Följande gång jag såg honom,
flera decennier senare,
var han märkt av kräftan,
hade krympt med hälften,
satt helst tyst och lyssnade.
Först fick han problem
med finskan, sen började
modersmålet vittra. Tumören
åt upp hans språk, en alien
som lurade under skallbenet.
. . .

(På månen råder tystnad,
eftersom ljudvågor
bara kan spridas i ett medium.
Men avsaknaden av atmosfär,
gör den samtidigt till en idealisk plats
för att undersöka solvinden, strömmarna
av subatomära partiklar.)
. . .

*Mängden vatten är konstant.*

## XVI

Some more debris floating
about: one summer's day
a few years after
Neil Armstrong made
the first footprint near
the south-western shore
of the Sea of Tranquillity,
I saw my uncle, the ship's engineer,
park his bronze Opel Manta
in the yard, get out and
walk towards us, standing in
the garage doorway. A wolfish
grin lit up his face.
Aviator's glasses, booming
        baritone.
. . .

(It will take ten million years
for the constant rain
of micrometeorites
to churn the uppermost
half-inch of lunar soil.
This means that the footprint
should last a million years,
maybe two.)

## XVII

Next time I saw him,
several decades later,
he was marked by disease,
had shrunk to half his size,
preferred to sit quiet and listen.
First he lost his Finnish,
then his mother tongue
began to crumble. The tumour
ate his language, an alien
burrowing inside his skull.
. . .

(On the Moon there is silence
because sound waves
can only travel in a medium.
But the absence of an atmosphere
makes it ideal for monitoring
the solar wind, streams
of subatomic particles.)
. . .

*The amount of water is constant.*

## XVIII

**Fråga**:
Vad betyder egentligen trösta?

**Svar**:
Redan då jorden skapades
för fem miljarder år sen
fanns vattnet bundet i
mineraler i jordens inre.
. . .

## XIX

(Odens häst *Sleipner*,
fornisländska Sleipnir –
'hal', 'halkig' –
kunde rusa fram
snabbare än någon
annan häst, på marken,
i luften, till havs.)
. . .

*Hörde min egen andning,*
harklade frustade
*Hörde min egen andning*
I ögonvrån
skuggor med nosande hundar,
ingen ropade åt mig,
trängde genom ytan
        (här/nu).

## XX

Valde denna gång att
jogga i motsatt riktning,
förbi elverket, över bron,
längs Metviksgatan.
. . .

Ett tjocknande
flimmer
i gatlyktornas koronor;
gångbanan pudrad,
på sina ställen såphal.

Hur springer man i halka?

## XVIII

**Question:**
What does comforting really mean?

**Answer:**
When our planet was created
five billion years ago,
water was already bound in
minerals inside the Earth.

. . .

## XIX

(Odin's horse *Sleipnir* –
'slippy', 'slippery'
in Old Icelandic –
could travel faster
than any other horse,
on the ground, in
the air, on water.)

. . .

*Heard my own breathing,*
wheezing snorting
*Heard my own breathing*
In the corner of my eye,
shadows with dogs sniffing,
no one shouting at me,
breaking through the surface
      (here/now).

## XX

This time I chose to jog
in the opposite direction,
passing the power station,
crossing the bridge, then
along Metviksgatan.
. . .

A thickening
haze
in the halo of the streetlamps;
pavements powdered,
slippery as soap in places.

How do you run on ice?

*XXI*

Yorkshire är täckt av vatten
och Whernside är en ö.

(Ljussvärta, bländljus, nova)
. . .

*Hon räfsade i strömmen,*
*längs med och på tvären.*
*Vid räfsningen på snedden,*
*kom det upp ett knippe lemmar*
*i den järnpinnade räfsan.*
. . .

Yorkshire är täckt av vatten
och Whernside är en ö.

Mängden vatten är konstant.
. . .

(Jorden snurras av hovar)

*Några noter*

1. I: 'Borden här är…' Peter Didsbury, 'A Gothic Yard', *That Old-Time Religion*.
2. II: 'Herakleitos berättade ofta…' Marcus Aurelius, *Självbetraktelser*.
3. VII: Marko kunde inte komma med den dagen på grund av arbete.
4. XXI: 'Hon räfsade i strömmen…' Bearbetat utdrag ur *Kalevala*, XV.
5. XXI: ' Jorden snurras…' Bearbetad version av en rad ur Torsten Petterssons diktsamling *Det finns inget annat*.

## XXI

Yorkshire is covered with water
and Whernside is an island.

(Black blaze, blaze blind, nova)

. . .

*She raked the river,*
*along and across;*
*as she was raking slantwise,*
*a bundle of limbs got stuck*
*in the iron-pronged rake.*

. . .

Yorkshire is covered with water
and Whernside is an island.

The amount of water is constant.

. . .

(The Earth is spun by hooves)

## *Some notes*

1. I: 'The tables here…' Peter Didsbury, 'A Gothic Yard', *That Old-Time Religion*.
2. II: 'Heraclitus often told us…' Marcus Aurelius, *Meditations*, translated by Gregory Hays.
3. VII: Marko couldn't join us that day because of work obligations.
4. XXI: 'She raked the river…' Adapted from *The Kalevala*, XV.
5. XXI: 'Jorden snurras av hovar…' Adapted from a poem by Torsten Pettersson, in *Det finns inget annat* (*There is nothing else*).

## Kath on Carita

Everywhere Carita goes she knows someone. 'I have a friend', she prefaces lots of stories, or 'I worked with them', or 'we did a programme'.

She also has a habit of disappearing. She would get in a lift on an upper floor and then not reappear at the bottom.

'I met a friend,' she would start, when we tracked her down.

We met briefly in 2001 at the Vasa Littfest. In 2004 we met again, and rapidly started talking.

Talking to Carita as we rattled along in her car, on the way to various readings, she told me that she thought the Swedish-speaking Finns of Ostrobothnia were a bit like the Irish of Finland. Coming from a large family, there were always stories – about the lost twin, about her mother giving birth, about the Finnish-speaking grandmother, about people driving their cars into ditches, about watching for fairies in midsummer, about children imagining tree spirits. Alongside the talking was the continuous crafting of the work – always the stubborness, holding out for the words she believed in, whether they were fashionable or not, knowing that things came around again and that what's worth doing can take a long time.

We laughed a lot, ate onion soup. She arranged tours for us, took us round her local museum, guided us into tasting Finnish food.

In later months: 'Forget the cleaning, forget the mess,' she'd tell me in emails, when I got overwhelmed by domestica. 'I hope you don't have too many 'must-dos'.'

I love the way Carita is fascinated by everybody and everything, how she can talk to a small child and then somebody elderly, her enthusiasm, the way she comes laden with gifts, a big bulging bag, suggestions, arrangements for things that might interest us, invitations to tea with old friends.

On her visit to England in 2004 we enjoyed a Turkish bath and sauna in Harrogate and took the waters in the Pump Museum (after a festive glass of mulled wine). Delighted by everything, she was interested in things that go unnoticed, snapping the William Morris wallpaper on one of my cupboards, and vegetables that I'd been cutting up.

Generous with her interest and time, she makes other writers feel their work is valued. Like the other Finnish Interlanders, she's laboured at getting the translations right. Tack så mycket. Slainte!

# Lost and found
A water-tale in fragments

# Försvunnen, återfunnen
En vattensaga i fragment

Carita Nyström

*Det var en gång*

Inte är det av jord du är kommen.
Ur havets skum föddes du.

Stränder stiger och stränder sjunker.
Sjöar svämmar över, sjöar torkar ut, torkar in, försvinner.
Floder söker nya vägar, slammar igen.
Den gåtfulla sjön Lop Noor i Gobiöknen vandrar, än är den här än där.
Ibland sjunker den undan, dyker ner i ökensanden.
Sven Hedin sökte den på sina ökenfärder. Gav upp utmattad av törst.
Idag spränger man kärnladdningar i Lop Noors närhet.

Nu regnar det över Bangla Desh, över Vietnam och Kina.
Det regnar över Småland, Vörå, Cornwall och Haiti.
Floder svämmar över.
Oder Neisse, Me Kong, Donau, Vanda å och Vörå.
Dammar brister i Andalusien och Xian Jing.

Grönlandsisen smälter, tio centimeter varje år.

Syndafloden är över oss.

*Once*

We are not from earth and dust.
We come from sea.

Shores rise and fall.
Lakes overflow, lakes dry up, die out, vanish.
Rivers seek new outlets, then silt up.
Lake Lop Noor in the Gobi desert wanders, it´s here, then there.
Sinking away, resurging, diving down again into the desert sand.
Sven Hedin chased it on his expeditions, gave up exhausted by thirst.
Today they do nuclear testing by Lop Noor.

Rain falls on Bangladesh, on Vietnam and China.
Rain falls on Cornwall, Haiti, Ostrobothnia.
Rivers flood:
Oder Neisse, Mekong, Danube, Vanda and Ouze.
Dams break in Andalusia and Xian Jing.

The Greenland ice is melting. Ten centimetres each year.

Deluge is here.

*Under ytan*

En gång flöt jag i ett urvatten, skyddad av starka hinnor – med mig simmade där en annan. Våra händer snuddade ibland vid varandra. Ljuden från den yttre världen rörde vid våra halvt utvecklade trumhinnor.

Så kastades vi upp på land och ut i livet. Det var vinter. Det var snö och kallt. En mörklagd stad. Det var krig. Du klarade inte omställningen. Ännu söker jag ditt ansikte i mängden, förlorade tvillingbror. Den diffusa skulden blev kvar, sorgen som ingen visste var sorg.

Jag lärde mig simma under vattenytan. Fann mig förunderligt tillrätta i den gulgrönt skimrande världen därnere. Svävande kropp. Alla ljud så avlägsna. Inget gjorde ont. Jag var lycklig. Jag kunde simma.

Men någons hårda händer ville hålla mig kvar därnere, när jag skulle upp för att hämta luft?

En senkommen hämnd? Måste sedan alltid alltid försäkra mig om, att jag bottnade. Att fötterna fann fäste. Aldrig längre ut än så.

*

Jag håller kvar drömmen att alltid vara i begynnelsen. Att aldrig växa upp. Kanske tror jag, att jag ännu ligger i ett urhav väntande på att inta min form.
Är det att vara författare? Att alltid längta efter sin form.

Önskar ibland att jag slapp känslan av att ständigt ändra form, att flyta ut, rinna undan, blandas och beblandas. Att jag slipper känslan att jag är som vatten, genomskinlig, speglande allt i min omgivning. Vill jag då frysa till is? Eller torka ut?

*Under the surface*

Once I floated – another floated there with me. Sometimes our hands brushed each other. Sounds from the outer world touched lightly our nascent ear-drums.

Then we were thrown ashore and out into life. It was winter, snow and bitterly cold. There was a war. You didn´t survive the change and I am still looking for your face in the crowd, lost twin-brother. Guilt remained, grief no-one knew was grief.

I learned to swim under water, feeling at ease in that limegreen shimmering world. Soaring body. All sounds so distant, nothing could hurt me. I was happy, I could swim.

But hard hands wanted to keep me under when I surfaced for air. A late revenge? Afterwards I always made sure my feet found footholds. I never swam further out.

\*

Holding on to the dream of the beginning. Is that the same as never growing up? Believing you´re still drifting in a womb waiting for form.
Is that what being a writer is, always longing for the perfect form?

Sometimes I want rid of the feeling of changing, flowing out and away, mixing, blending. I don´t want to be like water, transparent, reflecting everything around me. But do I want to freeze to ice then?
Or dry out?

*En annan strand*

Som krigsbarn tältade jag med min svenska familj ute vid kusten någonstans nära Sundsvall. Jag minns doften av skog som blandades med doften av varm sand, jag minns sticket från granriset under våra tältbäddar och ljuset genom tältduken. Om natten suckade små vågor in mot stranden.

Mest konturskarpt minns jag vattenbrynet, där jag vadade dagarna i ända. Den ljusa sanden mörknade och blev hård och slätskimrande, där vattnet nådde den, den ändrade färg när vattnet drog sig tillbaka. Bottnen räfflades i vågiga kammar av vågskvalpet lite längre ut. Sandrevlar höjde sig likt kontinenter ur vattnet ännu längre ut och jag vadade ut till dem. Spiggarnas vassa miniatyrknivar stack mig i fotsulan, då jag trampade på dem.

Strandbrynet var en hel värld, som jag tog i besittning, den absorberade mig. Gjorde mig mycket lycklig. Den var tillräcklig för mig. De vuxnas rop nådde mig från en annan planet. Avlägsen var hemlängtan, borta minnet av de svarta tågen som rasslade genom natten, borta skräcken att just nu kunde bomben falla. Fanns han där tillsammans med mig, färdkamraten ur ett annat hav? Anade jag, att där långt borta på andra sidan vattnet låg ett annat land? Ett hem?

Där krig, här fred.

*In-between worlds*

As a war-child I camped with my Swedish family on the coast close to Sundsvall. I remember the scent of spruce, and the warm sand. The pine needles under our tent beds pricked my skin. Light sieved through the tent cloth. In the night there was the sobbing of waves.

Most sharply I remember the water´s edge, where I waded all day long. The sand darkened when water reached it, lightened when the waves fell back. Further out sandbanks rose like continents, I waded out to take possession of them. Sticklebacks pierced my footsoles like miniature knives.

The water´s edge, a whole world, absorbed me completely. It was enough for me. Grown-ups shouted from their distant planet. My homesickness was gone. Black trains clattering through the night were gone, and the dread that the bombs would fall. There was only sea, sand, waves and me. Perhaps my long lost twin. And far away another shore. Home?

Peace here, war there.

*Simturer*

Tiden kom, när jag flöt utan rädsla. Jag kunde inte få nog av att simma. Kroppen sträcktes ut, och kröp ihop, sträcktes, kröp ihop, sträcktes. Vattnet forsade runt mun, näsa, ögon, öron. Frasade runt kroppen, susade i öronen, min häftiga andhämtning. In ovan vattnet, ut i ett flås under vattnet. Luftbubblor kittlade mina kinder.

Ständigt fann jag nya ställen att korsa med långa kraftiga simtag.

Intill fjärden i fars gamla by hade vi ett sommarviste. Fjärden var en djup skåra i landskapet, ett spår av inlandsisens färd över jordplanet. Inte en sten i hela fjärden, jo en, mitt i faret längre ut. Den kände alla till.

Jag korsade fjärden från norr till söder och tillbaka. Sedan i vida trianglar, kvadrater. En hel sommar simmade jag kors och tvärs över Österfjärden, från strand till strand. Ner mot vattnet sluttade magra ängar med blåklocka och gulmåra mellan gråstenar, strandbodar och gistvallar, där då ännu fisknät hängdes till tork. Men aldrig landade jag på stenen mitt i faret.

*Vattennyheter*

Läser i söndagstidningen att en man bestämt sig för att simma från Sverige till Finland i sommar, utrustad med dykardräkt, simbräde, glukostabletter. Han säger att turen kommer att ta tio till femton dagar i anspråk. Myndigheterna ber honom se upp för de stora passagerarfärjorna. Dessa kan inte, upplyser man, väja för något så litet som en människa.

I samma tidning läser jag, att man bland Yorubafolket tror, att om din tvilling dör vid födseln tar han med sig halva din själ. I en sekundsnabb glimt förstår jag mig själv.

*A swim memoir*

Time came when I floated without fear. I couldn´t have enough of swimming. My body stretched, crouched, stretched, crouched, stretched. Water gushed over mouth, nose, eyes, ears. Rippled round my body, buzzed in my ears. My panting breath. Air bubbles tickled my cheeks.

I always found new waters to cross with long strokes.

Close to the inlet in my father´s home village we had a summer-place. The bay was a deep scar in the landscape, formed by the force of the inland ice moving over the earth´s surface. Only one rock in the entire bay, further out in the middle of the bay, hidden under the water.

I crossed the bay from south to north and back. Swam in wide triangles, then in squares. The entire summer I swam in all directions crisscross, from shore to shore. Meagre meadows slanted down, covered in carpets of harebells and lady´s bedstraw among granite rocks. I never landed on that rock in the bay though.

*Water news*

In Sunday´s newspaper I read about a man who this summer plans to swim from Sweden to Finland in a wet suit, with swimming floats and glucose pills. He says the swim will take from ten to fifteen days. The authorities have asked him to stay clear of the shipping lanes. Ferries cannot, they inform him, veer for something as small as a human being.

In the same paper I find a notice about the Yoruba belief, that if one twin dies at birth he takes half the soul of the other with him. In a flash I seem to understand myself.

*Ön i havet*

Havet flyttar vår lilla sandstrand som det vill
Tidigt om sommaren kommer vi ut till ön, undrar:
var är sanden i år? vad har havet hittat på?

En anspråkslös smal strimma i vattenbrynet
eller en duktig vall högre upp där gräset tar vid?
Varje vår bjuder havet på nya överraskningar.

Alar som brutits av isen ligger som vitnade ben
i strandsvallet, havtornsbuskage vandrar ut mot vattnet
som drar sig tillbaka, gör plats för strandängens salta
   örter.

Högsommarn förvandlar denna steniga strand
kröner den med älggräs och valeriana.

*En ö på land*

– Så, ni skall bygga i Finnviken, sa den gamla kvinnan
   leende,
enda stället här i byn, där man kan odla vete. Hon visste.
Huset står nu på kullen som en gång var en ö.

För fyrahundra år sedan låg ännu Finnviken
under vatten, väntade på sin förvandling till åkerjord.
Idag kämpar vi mot sly, skog som vill ta över.

I ljusa sommarkvällar tycker jag mig se dem ro de grunda
   vattnen,
lägga ut sina nät på våra åkrar, där en gång braxen, gädda, id
   och sik
simmat i de näringsrika vattnen, en ymnighet av fisk.

Tog de i land nån gång, dansade på hällarna
som huset vårt är grundat på.

*The island in the sea*

Each year the sea moves our tiny beach as it pleases.
Arriving in the island early summer we always wonder:
Where´s our beach this year?

A modest strand of sand on the water´s edge or
a good-sized bank higher up where grass grows?
Each year the sea offers new surprises.

Whitened bones of alder broken by the ice lie licked
by salty waves; sea buckthorn marches waterwards
and sea withdraws yielding space for salty herbs.

High summer transforms this barren shore
with heady showers of valerian.

*The island on land*

– So, you´re building in Finn Bay, the old woman said,
the only place you can grow wheat in our village.
On a hillock once an island the house now stands.

Four hundred years ago Finn Bay still lay
under water, waiting to transform into fertile soil.
And now we´re fighting the forest from taking over.

On summer nights I think I see them row the shallow waters,
setting their nets in our fields where once pike and perch
swam in rich waters, feeding the poor village.

Maybe they paused to dance on the solid rock
our house is founded on.

*Sommarregn*

Det regnar över huset, regnar och regnar. Hela denna sommar regnar bort. Och det gröna fyller allt, det fyller min trädgård, det tränger in i huset. Det klättrar upp längs väggarna, nästlar sig in genom fönsterspringor, dränker sängarna, borden, stolarna. Vi gror in. Det regnar.

Vi överrumplas av ett åskväder med hagelbyar och ösregn i släptåg. Hagel, tumstora, bombarderar våra fönsterrutor. Skräckslagna söker vi oss till rummets mitt, då skottelden känns in på bara skinnet. Efter några minuters ösregn är vår uppfart en skummande flod. Vattnet vill återta land.


*Orrmoan*

Högt uppe på en höjd inne i skogen ligger den,
klapperstranden, djävulsåkern. Och där intill
tre djupa gropar, en till hälften bortgrävd jungfrudans.

Här rastade i forna dagar sälfångstmän som kommit
över havet, fiskade, fångade, satt vid sina eldar
och väntade kanhända bättre väder, förlig vind

och de beträdde jungfrudansens labyrint gång på gång
för att besvärja stormar, rovdjur, Ran i djupet, Ägirs maka,
hon den försåtliga som lägger sina nät för mänskofiskar.

Då skogen nedanför var ung sågs havet härifrån
blåblankt på klara dagar över unga björkar, nyutslagna.
Stig varsamt nu mellan sten, kråkris och lummer.

*Flood*

It´s raining, it´s raining non-stop. The whole summer rains away. Green moisture fills my garden, forces itself into the house, climbs up walls, creeps over the beds. We are choking on green. Fear of flooding grows.

One day we are taken by surprise by a thunderstorm followed by violent hail and downpour. Hailstones big as thumbs bombard our windows. We are in the line of fire, draw together in the middle of the room. A few minutes pass and our drive is transformed into a fast flowing riverbed. Is the sea taking back the land?

*Orrmoan*

    Deep in the forest on a hill lies the shingled shore,
    the devil´s field. And close by three deep pits
    and a stone labyrinth, half dug out.

    Two thousand years ago, they say, seal-hunters
    rested here from the sea, catching fish, sitting by the fires
    waiting for calm weather and fair winds for sailing.

    Treading patiently the labyrinth paths they would
    beseech stormy winds, wild beasts, and Ägir´s wife,
    treacherous Ran who sets her nets for fishermen.

    On clear days the open sea blazes blue
    above young birches in new leaf.
    Step lightly now on stones, crowberry and moss.

*Läsestycken*

Det händer ibland, de vintrar då vattenståndet sjunker drastiskt, att hålrum bildas under isen. När vattnet drar sig undan helt kan man vistas därnere om man borrar ett lagom stort hål i isen. Det gjorde Too-Ticki, den vintervana, i Trollvinter. Min son och jag var lika lyckliga över denna oväntade vändning i läsningen. Vilken upptäckt det var, utrymmet under isen, dit boken förde oss.

Så var det Uleåborgsgubben i Wacklins 'Hundrade minnen', han som försvann med sin kälke i hög fart in under isen över älven. Alla trodde honom förlorad, men gubben hade vandrat under isen till en vak, som han mindes skulle finnas längre upp längs älvfåran. Där dök han upp glatt ropande. Bara stövlarna var våta och han kunde berätta om det låga isvalvet, där han gått framåtböjd på isglatta stenar i dunkelt ljus. Och den goda mamsell Wacklin fångade in honom med sin penna, så att vi nu kan höra honom hojta till vid nedre loppet av Ule älv. Tvåhundra år senare. Själv tyckte han inte saken var så märkvärdig.

*I fälan*

Alla historier om äventyr i fälan, som jag hört sedan jag flyttade hit. Om veckorna ute i Bottniska Vikens vita land. Om förberedelser, som hela byn deltog i. Om provianten, kilovis av bröd och smör, torkat kött och brännvin att hålla liv och värme uppe genom kalla nätter och dagar. Om sockor, tröjor, fårskinnsfällar, spelkort, skidor. Om lodbössor, gevär. Den vita dräkten att dölja sig i för villebrådet. Sedan de tunga kropparna blödande på kritvit is.

De berättade om isbröten höga som hus, som krossat jägare och båtar. Köldknäppar som låst alla vatten och tvingat jägarna att vänta i sina öppna båtar. Isflak som lossnat med båtar och mannar och drivit söderut. Några blev borta för alltid. Ett isflak stort som två åkrar lossnade medan fäljägarna låg och sov. De fördes med havsvinden söderut mot nya skär. Då de vaknade hade de strandat vid en strand, de aldrig sett förut.

Men ingen här har hört om sälfolket. Hur de som drunknat förvandlas i havet, blir sälar. Och kan återvända, kasta sälhamnen och dansa på klipporna vid fullmåne. Hemsöka sina kära.

*Readings*

Winters when the water level sinks drastically cavities form under the ice. When the water withdraws completely, you can go down if you bore a wide enough hole in the ice. Too-Ticki, familiar with winter, went fishing there. My son and I were delighted by this unexpected turn in the story. What a discovery the book offered us; that space under the ice

And that old man in Oulu in Sara Wacklin´s 'A Hundred Memories'; he who vanished with his sledge under the river ice. Everyone thought him lost, but instead he started walking under the ice towards an ice-hole he remembered. There he emerged with happy shouts. Only his boots were wet and he told the stunned crowd that he crouched under the low vault in semi-darkness, treading on the icy stones. And there the honourable Miss Wacklin caught him with her pen. Two hundred years later we can hear him shouting at the lower run of Oulunjoki. He didn´t find the whole thing remarkable at all.

*Seal hunting*

They told me stories of adventures on the ice, of weeks spent out on the frozen Kvarken, hunting seals. How they prepared themselves, the whole village working together. Of the supplies of bread and butter, dried meat and liquor to sustain them through cold nights and days. Of socks and sweaters, playing cards and skis. The guns. The white they wore to make themselves invisible. And then the heavy bodies bleeding on the ice, colouring the snow.

They told me of ice-floes hovering up to the skies like palaces of ice, or drifting away, southwards with boats and men. Some vanishing forever. A floe once set adrift with northern winds while the men were asleep in the boat. They woke up stranded on a far island they had never seen before. Were found and saved.

But none of them had ever heard of Silkies. How those who drowned turned into seals and could return, cast off their seal skins, dance on the rocks at full moon. Haunting their loved ones.

*Saudade*

Havet häver sakta rytande,
överrumplar – kastar dig omkull i svallet,
doftar fräser väser suckar sakta – *saudade*
Portugals vemod glöder mörkt
som tårar, salt och blod

Jorden – röd under olivträd dignande till skörd
tiggerskan i svart – *misericordia*
visa barmhärtighet. Men inte golfarna, nej
inte de i vita kläder, som lätta fjädrar blåsta hit,
från ingenstans till ingenstans,
där elden sveder skogarna till svärta.

Tanken att vi är här denna höst
överrumplar, liksom skrattet, grönt som glädjen,
igenkännandet, historien – en röd sekund vårt liv –
minnet av en bror en syster
borta nu – snart också vi – som fjun av aska
                        över hav och jord.

*Styx*

Om natten har regnet
kristalliserats till stjärnor.
När morgonen kommer
virvlar de utanför fönstret.
Floden är svart, dess kalla vatten
flyter tungt. Karon förtöjde båten
helt nära huset. Tålmodigt väntar han
medan snöflingorna smälter på vattnet.
Han väntar på ännu en passagerare.

*Saudade*

The mighty sea, its muted roar,
astounds me – throws me down in the surf –
howling, hissing, sighing softly – saudade
sweet grief of Portugal, with a dark glow
the kin of tears, salt and blood

The earth – red under the olive trees, heavy with fruit
the beggar woman in black – misericordia –
show mercy. But not the golfers, not those
in white clothes, flown here like feathers
from nowhere to nowhere
somewhere the fire burnt the forests black.

Realising that we are here just now
astounds me, like laughter, green as joy,
the recognition, history – our life a red second –
memories of a brother or sister, gone now
– as we soon will be – white fluff of ashes
                              over sea and earth.

*Styx*

In the night the rain
crystallized into stars.
When morning came
they whirled outside the window.
A long journey lies ahead.
The river´s black and cold, its water
slowly runs. Charon tied his boat
close to the house. He´s patient,
watches snowflakes melt upon the water,
waits for another passenger.

*Marko on Adam*

When I first started translating Adam's 'Depth Soundings' for our readings in Finland, I was a bit scared of the task. It wasn't just the important details like whether or not I understood what 'blowing goats' means, but also that his metaphors are such borderline cases that once you touch them, you become genuinely paranoid about losing some of the original's reverberations. And I have to admit that when Adam sent the very first draft (or two versions of it actually) I was a bit uncertain as to what he was up to. I saw several different and similarly exciting directions the story could take but couldn't see a way they all could happen at once. But apparently for Adam, who always seems to be involved in about a hundred projects at the same time, this isn't a problem at all.

I'm still amazed at how 'Depth Soundings' works as well as it does. It's a combination of cool prose and vivid, intense poetry that at times has a slight archaic feel to it. Myth is there, in Beowulf and Breca and in the descent to the underworld, but is reinvented in the matter-of-fact world of Manchester commuters, hair straighteners and the World Service.

To me, this reflects something characteristically Adam. He is interested in classical music, he knows his history and mythology. But, perhaps due to his work in international drama projects, he always recognises the coexistence of different historical and cultural perspectives in the here and now. That's the potential Adam brings to everything he does, whether it's a multicultural writing project or a night out in a pub somewhere in Yorkshire or Finland.

Despite all the different elements, Adam's piece is perhaps closest to a classical story in this anthology. But it's a story told through several kinds of expression at once. There is a touch of drama, of course, and poetry with concrete yet dream-like metaphors, and prose that at times reads almost like a mystery novel. And the tragedy at the heart of the piece is so cruel that I feel vaguely guilty for being so fascinated by it.

# Depth Soundings

# Syvyysmittauksia

## Adam Strickson

*Yorkshire watermarks*

*Before the tale begins, I scribble notes about gloomy paths, swimming holes, weather forecasts, brass bands and distant tremors. I thrill to the rhythms of the Kalevala and simmer my words in Dante's sauna. Something is in the air, something is in the water, something rumbles…*

*Yorkshiren vesimerkkejä*

*Ennen kuin tarina alkaa, raaputan muistiinpanoja pahaenteisistä poluista, uima-aukoista, sääennusteista, puhallinorkestereista ja kaukaisista värähtelyistä. Pulahdan intensiivisen keskustelun vesiin ja poltan kynttilää pitkälle yöhön. Tärisen Kalevalan rytmeissä ja kiehutan sanojani Danten saunassa. Ilmassa on jotakin, vedessä on jotakin, jokin jyrisee maan alla…*

*Syvyysmittauksia*

Kun kuuntelee tärähdyksiä
Yorkshiren alla
aallot kaikuvat syvällä.
Mikrojäristyksiä, matalataajuisia, äänettömiä,
helppoja kuvitella

Päästäisen viimeinen hengenveto
luupissa, ikuisesti.

Kun kuuntelee tärähdyksiä
Yorkshiren alla
aallot kaikuvat,
kaukana ajassa, rajuja, äänettömiä,
helppoja kuvitella

Beowulf ja Breca
uivat kilpaa,
kisaavat Pohjanmerta.

Breca hukkuu.
Beowulf ajautuu rantaan
Suomen rannikolle

hengittää kuin päästäinen.

*Depth soundings*

When you listen for earthquakes
under Yorkshire
waves resonate deep underground:
microseisms, low frequency, unheard,
easy to imagine –

the last breath of a shrew
looped, replayed for ever.


When you listen for earthquakes
under Yorkshire
waves resonate:
distant in time, violent, unheard,
easy to imagine –

Beowulf and Breca
swim against each other,
race the North Sea.

Breca sinks.
Beowulf is laid ashore
on the coast of Finland

breathes like a shrew.

*Vain sateinen iltapäivä*

Numeroiden välissä,
kun orkesteri hengähtää,
asettelee sordiinejaan ja luistejaan,
kapellimestari kertoo vitsin
Lancashiresta,
vaikka se on pikemminkin
kuvaus Yorkshiresta:

Ja Jumala loi
hienoimman krikettijoukkueen,
hiekkaisimman hiekkarannan,
sinisimmän sinitaivaan,
vihreimmän laakson,
ylpeimmät ihmiset.

Kapellimestari
kohottaa kätensä.
Orkesteri löytää

jotakin vaan
ei nuottia.

Sen sijaan he puhaltavat,
löytävät vain ääntä:
tuulen vihellyksen
läpi West Nabin,
aallot Sandsendissä,
pärskeen suhinan
Gaping Ghyllissä,
sateen piiskeen
Haworthin pappilassa,
ujeltavat aukot
kuivamuuratuissa seinissä.

*Another rainy afternoon*

Between numbers,
while the band get their breath,
adjust their mutes and slides,
the conductor tells a joke
about Lancashire,
which is mostly a description
of Yorkshire:

And God created
the finest cricket team,
the sandiest of sandy beaches,
the bluest of blue skies,
the greenest of dales,
the proudest of people.

The conductor
raises his hand.
The band strike up
but do not arrive
at a note.

Instead, they blow,
find only sounds:
the whistle of wind
through West Nab,
waves at Sandsend,
the whirr of spray
in Gaping Ghyll,
the lash of rain
on Haworth Parsonage,
the swish of gaps
in drystone walls.

*Tämä vetinen tarina alkaa paikassa jossakin
Yorkhiressa, jossakin kylää pienemmässä.*

## Seitsemän kaivon kylä

*Asettuminen veteen ja pimeään*

> Vilu mulle virttä virkkoi
> sae saatteli runoja
> linnut liitteli sanoja
> puien latvat lausehia
>
> *Kalevala 1: Runo*

Matthew ja Rose saapuvat tyttärensä Rowanin kanssa tähän seitsemän kaivon kylään marraskuun alussa. He haluavat aloittaa alusta 'eräässä maailman pimeistä paikoista'. Vedet solisevat heidän jalkojensa alla, mihin ikinä he astuvatkaan, talojen sisällä ja ulkona. Kun hän sulkee silmänsä, likaiset kangaspuut kalisevat kankaankutojan ikkunan takana.

Kylässä ei ole pubia, kauppaa, ei kirkkoa. Viktorian aikainen koulu, korkea kuin kallio ja juuri uudelleen avattu kuivalahon hävittämisen jälkeen, takertuu kukkulankylkeen. Harottava hautausmaa, jyrkkä kuin heivaamaisillaan muistomerkit alas laaksoon, makaa muurinrykelmän takana. Kiemuraiset polut kulkevat sukkelaan, sopivammat aaseille kuin nelipyöräisille. Ne päättyvät jyrkkiin heinäpeltoihin, jossa hevoset makaavat, odottaen sadetta.

Matthew, Rose ja Rowan astuvat halkeilevaan ja vinoon taloon, joitakin sen huoneista ei ole valaistu aikoihin. He tuovat valon, sähköjohtoja, asennuksia, hehkulamppujen vaihtamisen, he pitävät pimeää poissa.

Laaksossa, kaukana talon alapuolella, kokkovalkeat palavat läpi talven. Kypäräpäiset miehet purkavat Titanic -myllyn ulkovajoja, liian myöhään rakennettuja, tuhansien kankaankutojien hetkellisiä asumuksia, tuhoon tuomittuja kuin laiva, jonka mukaan paikka nimettiin. Sitä raivataan asunnoiksi. Huhutaan ravintolasta, jossa on pianisti ja suuret portaat, kopio tuosta kuuluisasta, monen sylen syvyydessä makaavasta. Manchesterissa

*This watery tale begins in a Yorkshire place, something less than a village.*

# The hamlet of seven wells

*Settling in to water and darkness*

> *The cold told a tale to me*
> *the rain suggested poems…*
> *the birds added words*
> *the treetops phrases…*
>
> Kalevala 1: In the Beginning

Matthew and Rose, and their daughter Rowan, come to this hamlet of seven wells at the beginning of November. They choose to make their new start in 'one of the dark places of the earth'. The waters gurgle beneath their feet wherever they step, inside and outside the houses. When Matthew shuts his eyes, looms of grimy wood clatter behind the weavers' windows.

There is no pub, no shop, no church. A Victorian school, high as a cliff, newly reopened after the killing of dry rot, clings to the hillside. A tangled graveyard, so steep it threatens to lob memorial slabs into the valley below, lies behind a tumble of fallen walls. The narrow, winding paths climb rapidly, as if expecting donkeys rather than four wheel drives. They end in steep hayfields where horses lie down, waiting for rain.

Matthew and Rose and Rowan come to a house cracked and bent, a house in which some rooms have not been lit for a long time. They bring light: rewiring, installing, forever changing blown bulbs to keep out the darkness.

In the valley, far below the house, bonfires burn all winter. Men in hard hats are demolishing the outer sheds of Titanic Mill, built too late, briefly home to thousands of weavers, doomed like the ship it was named after. The men will hack it into apartments: there are rumours of a restaurant with pianist and grand staircase, a replica of the famous one so many fathoms under the ocean. Manchester commuters and the retired will live on an island

työssä käyvät ja eläkeläiset uneksivat ilon ja mukavuuksien saarekkeesta, kanaalin suoruuden ja kiemuraisen joen ahtaumassa. Veden kolminaisuuden täyttää uima-allas.

    Joskus tulee mies valkoisella pakettiautollaan vastapäisen autiotalon pihaan ja tyhjentää vaivihkaa kuormansa läiskälle paljasta maata. Seuraa roihu, joka pakottaa Matthewin sulkemaan ikkunat palavien maalipurkkien mustalta savulta. Sen hiottu sulosointuskaala tunkee läpi kaksinkertaisten ikkunoiden. Usein sataa viikkoja.

    Kaivo pilkistää puutarhan yläosasta, kumimaisten begonioiden saartama synkkä kaukalo, murattien ja villin karhunvatukan puoliksi peittämä. Muovinen pesukarhu tuijottaa vajan ikkunalaudalta. Eukalyptus on väärässä maassa.

    Kesä tulee sopertaen. Päiväkurjenmiekat kestävät päivän. Ikikarsimattomat puut, plataanit ja saarnet, luovat kukkapenkkien ylle upean katoksen, pitävät aurinkoa, jotta saniaiset ja etanat saavat kukoistaa. Grilli on allas ruostetta. Matthew vetää vihreän peipon kissan suusta; se oli vaaninut kuusaman vieressä, päästyään ulos ensimmäistä kertaa päiviin, nautti tauosta sateiden välissä, tappaen.

of pleasure and convenience, stranded between the straightness of the canal and the swirl of the river. The trinity of waters will be completed by a swimming pool.

Sometimes, a man comes with a white van to the deserted house opposite and shiftily dumps the contents on a patch of earth. Then there's a closer bonfire and Matthew shuts the windows against the black smoke of burning paint cans. The ups and downs of Euphonium scales penetrate the double-glazing. Often, it rains for weeks.

A well lurks at the top of the garden, a dark trough bordered with rubbery bergenias, half hidden by ivy and rogue brambles. A plastic racoon stares from the windowsill of the shed. The eucalyptus is in the wrong country.

Summer splutters in. Day irises last a day. The never lopped giant weeds of sycamore and ash make a great canopy over the flowerbeds, keeping out the sun, so ferns and snails thrive.

The barbecue is a sink of rust. Matthew pulls a greenfinch out of the cat's mouth; the cat was waiting by the honeysuckle, out for the first time for days, enjoying the gap in the rains, killing.

*Huone maan alla*

**Vesi**
Naapurit kertoivat heille. Kerran heidän kellarinsa laudoitettiin umpeen. Sanomalehtiä pursuavan talon alla oli kasapäin viiniä: makeaa voikukkaa, hapanta raparperia ja muita, kukkuloiden marjoista valmistettuja, mutta kaikki menneet etikaksi vuosia sitten. Heidän kellarinsa pisaroi kuin kalkkikiviluola.

Kun he ensimmäisen kerran katsoivat taloa ja laskeutuivat kivirappusia, he näkivät kellarin tietämättä tästä kaikesta. Pitkä pöytä oli houkutteleva ja tuoreen sokerikakun tuoksu leijui ilmassa. Synkkä kuva neidosta, ritarista ja lohikäärmeestä koristi hellyttävän mauttomasti yhtä seinää. He eivät huomanneet laattoihin porattuja reikiä, joiden läpi vesi sai tihkua pois. He eivät nähneet sienten pilkistystä jalkalistan ja lattian välistä. Kellari puhui heille piikiven punaisena ja auringonkeltaisena. Sen Yorkshire -juuret oli visusti peitetty meksikolaisella aksentilla. He eivät kuulleet maanalaisen virran solinaa, kuplintaa lattian alla.

Sen jälkeen, kun he olivat asettuneet taloksi, Matthew asettui usein makuulle, painoi korvansa laattoja vasten ja tunsi veden kohinan.

**Tuli**
Heidän kellarissaan on puulämmitin, se on mustaa valurautaa ja varustettu kahdella karstaisella puolalla, jotka estävät halkojen tippumisen tuhkapesään. Kun lämmittimessä ei ole tulta, voi sen sisällä nähdä The Three Billy Goats Gruff -tekstin kohokirjaimin. Kun se loimuaa, hahmot häilähtelevät seinämällä ennen kuolemaansa. Polttoputa varten Matthew ottaa esiin Pace Egg –korin ja kerää pudonneita risuja saarnien alta. Palavan puun savu takertuu kaikkeen yläkerroksessa, jopa huilunsoittoon.

**Vesi**
Tämä on kesätarina: tuli on sammunut. Kuuntele vettä.

*A room underground*

*Water*
Their neighbours told them once their cellar was boarded up. Under a house piled high with newspapers, it was stacked with wine: sweet dandelion, sour rhubarb, others brewed from berries on the hills, all gone to vinegar years before. Their cellar dripped like a limestone cave.

When they first viewed the house and came down the stone stairs, they saw the cellar without this knowledge. The long table was inviting; the smell of a freshly baked sponge egged the air. Black cartoons of a lady, a warrior and a dragon lovingly decorated one wall. They did not notice holes drilled through the flags for water to seep away. They did not see the gills of fungi winking in the gap between skirting board and floor. The cellar spoke to them in firestone red and sun yellow. Its Yorkshire origins were thickly disguised by its Mexican accent. They did not hear the underground stream gurgle and bubble beneath the floor.

After they moved in, Matthew loved to lie down, put his ear to the flags and feel the rush of water.

*Fire*
Their cellar has a log burning fire, black cast iron, with two crusted spanners to stop logs falling through to the ash pan. When it is unlit, they can look inside and see The Three Billy Goats Gruff cavort in relief. When it blazes, 'soldiers' flicker on the back wall before they die. For tinder, Matthew takes out the Pace Egg basket and collects twigs from under the ash trees. The smell of wood smoke gets into everything on the floor above, even flute music.

*Water*
This is a summer story: the fire is out. Listen to the water.

## Toukokuun riitit

*Sukuvirttä suoltamahan*
*lajivirttä laulamahan*

*Kalevala 1: Runo*

*'Tytär, kultaseni,*
*läheinen kaukainen tytär,*
*joka neljäntoista vuoden jälkeen*
*sanoi kerran*
*"en TUNNE sinua",*
*anna minun kertoa heille, kuinka sinut menetin,*
*menetin kerran, menetin kahdesti*
*onnettomilla mailla ja vesillä*
*Pohjoisessa.'*

Sade hellittää. Kuukausi on toukokuu.
Tähtimerkki: helleskorpioni. Todellinen
paahtamoinen: kuuma, humiseva toukokuun
päivä seitsemän kaivon kylässämme.
Piippolimakotilot parittelevat hekumallisina
takertumina, itsepölyttävät unikot siementävät
ilman häpyä, selkäpanssaroidut armeijat ryömivät
plataaninlehtien ja saarnen siipihedelmien katveesta
valmiina toimintaan.

Tämä on lähtöpäivien lähtöpäivä
jossa olipa kerran -aika alkaa taas,
viimeinen koulupäivä
ensimmäinen päivä elämää.

Viimeinen koulupäivä on hulluutta
Clairelle ja Mollylle ja Marthalle ja Ninalle ja Lilylle ja
Rowanberrysparkle1@hotmail.comille.
Kyse ei ole vain univormun häpäisystä:
leveät kauluskäänteet, avonaiset napit,
suuret kravattisolmut juuri rintojen yläpuolella.
Kyse on univormun vaihdosta
rah-rah –mekkoihin, punaisiin sukkahousuihin,
pinkkehin paljettikenkiin
ja täpläsukkiin.

Rowanberrysparklella on viimeisenä koulupäivänä
valkoinen paita ja kuusi tuntia myöhemmin kotona

# Rites of May

*reeling off a tale of kin*
*singing a tale of kind*

*Kalevala 1: In the Beginning.*

*'Daughter, sweetheart,*
*close distant daughter,*
*who after fourteen years*
*once said*
*"I don't KNOW you",*
*let me tell them how I lost you,*
*lost you once, lost you twice*
*in the luckless land and waters*
*of the North.'*

The rain lets up. It's the month of May. Star sign: Scorchio. A real scorcher: a hot, humming May day in our village of seven wells. Pond snails are doing it in sexy clutches, self-seeding poppies spill seed irresponsibly, carapaced armies creep out from under the mulch of sycamore leaves and ash keys looking for action.

It is the leaving day of leaving days
where once upon a new time begins:
the last day of school,
the first day of life.

The last day at school is tribal
for Claire and Molly and Martha and Nina and Lily and
Rowanberrysparkle1@hotmail.com.
It's not just the abuse of uniform:
wide lapels, undone buttons,
the large knots of ties worn just above the breasts.
It's the abandonment of uniform for
rah-rah skirts, red tights, pink sequinned shoes
and spotty dotty socks.

Rowanberrysparkle wears her white shirt to her
last day at school and, six hours later, wears it
home, adorned with ritual scrawls felt penned
across cuffs, sleeves, back and front, even the
bottom of the front where an arrow points

hänellä on se yllään, se on tahrittu rituaalituherruksin pitkin hihansuita, hihoja, edestä ja takaa, jopa etupuolen helma, jossa nuoli osoittaa alas ja teksti selittää 'Auki ympäri vuorokauden'. Se ei ole totta. Mies on hänen isänsä; hän tietää, ettei se ole totta. Hän ei tarvitse muidenkaan kirjoitusten tietoa:

```
Hyvä perse.
Mun tissi.
Onnea matkaan kulta.
Sexy mo to! Yo!
Rowan runkkaa vuohia.
Rave for the P/F.
Faarbur Sexi!
Nähään puistossa. T: Copster.
```

Hän ei ymmärrä kaikkea, mutta on huolissaan Copsterin ja tyttärensä tapaamisesta puutarhassa. Puutarha on vaarallinen paikka.

*Illalla ystävät tapaavat puolikypsien makkaroiden ja pullotettujen sinisten koktailien merkeissä grillijuhlissa Greenillä. Mukavaa, kännistä hauskaa on. Kaikki lähtevät. Puolenyön maissa Matthew ja Rose menevät petiin. Rowan hakee taskulampun ja siivoaa sotkun.*

towards her front bottom with the legend, 'Open all hours'. This is not true. He is her father; he knows this is not true. He does not need the information revealed by other words:

```
Fine bit ov ass.
My tit.
Good luck hun.
Sexy mo to! Yo!
Rowan blows goats.
Rave for the P/F.
Faarbur Sexi!
See ya in the garden. Luv Copster.
```

He does not know what it all means but is worried by the thought of Copster meeting her in the garden. The garden is a dangerous place.

*In the evening, the schoolfriends meet for a barbecue of half cooked sausages and bottled blue cocktails at the top of the Green. A good and boozy time is had by all. Everyone leaves. Around midnight, Matthew and Rose go to bed. Rowan takes a torch to clear up the mess…*

# Kylmässä helvetissä, tiheikössä

*Hiustensuoristajat*

> *Suan seinähän sivalti,*
> *Harjan paiskoi patsahasen*
>
> *Kalevala 12: Runo*

Joka yö hän kuulee laivauutiset, sitten kansallishymnin, sitten vihdoin uutisia maailmalta. Yhden jälkeen hänen korvakuulokkeensa on kytketty rosoisiin uutisiin Talibaneista, Sudanista, kaappauksista ja nälänhädästä. Hän yrittää turruttaan kauhunsa tarinoilla joukkohaudoista ja naulapommeista, mutta hänen päässään kiertää ikään kuin soraa, tuskan ja väsymyksen rohina. Puoli kolmelta hän vaihtaa CD-soittimeen ja yrittää musiikkia: Satie – liian laguunimaista; sitten Gabrielin puhaltimia, harrasta tavaraa – viritettyjä enkeleitä, täyteläisiä kyyneleitä ja niin edelleen, mutta se ei lennätä nyt mihinkään. Unettomuus ja suru painavat häntä maahan, mutta hän soittaa levyn uudelleen ja uudelleen ja uudelleen, kunnes fanfaarit puhaltavat hänet uneen. Ei lohduttavaa messua, ei kupoleita, ei venetsialaisia kanaaleita. Uni paiskaa hänet tyttären huoneen sekasortoon, kertakäyttölautasia, huulipunaa, rytätty koulutehtävä maksan toiminnasta, tuherrettu teksti: "yksin pitkin jäistä katua", ja sydänkuvioinen sukka. Hänen liila, tähtikuvioinen pyjamansa on myttynä lattialla. Housujen alta hän löytää hiustensuoristajan kylmänä, mutta kytkettynä pistorasiaan. Kun hän ottaa sen käteensä, se on äkkiä kuuma, vuotaa verta, se leviää kuin tulva viemäriputkista nilkkoihin saakka. Hän hutaa nähdessään tyttärensä kasvot, jotka kelluvat epäselvinä aaltoilevalla pinnalla ja huutavat mykkinä: "Isä! Isä!". Sitten hän on poissa.

*Painajainen ei suostu katoamaan. Aamulla Matthew huomaa, ettei Rowan ole huoneessaan. Olennot seinillä uivat arvoitusta. Kun Matthew vihdoin seuraavana yönä nukahtaa, hän tajuaa tulleensa kutsutuksi Greenin laelle.*

# In cold hell, in thicket

## *The hair straighteners*

> *He flung the comb at the wall*
> *the brush he hurled at the post…*
>
> Kalevala 12: A Bond Broken.

Each night, he hears the shipping news, then the national anthem, then – at last – the World Service. Just past one, he's ear-plugged in to tinny news of Taliban, Sudan, kidnappings and starvation. He hopes to press his horror down with mass graves or nail bombs but something like gravel whirls in his head, a grinding noise of pain and tiredness. At half past two, he changes to the CD player and tries music: Satie – too lagoon-like; then Gabrieli's brass, the holy stuff – toned angels, voluptuous tears – but it flies him nowhere. He's weighed down with insomnia and sadness but he plays it again and again and again until it fanfares him to sleep.

No comforting Mass, no domes, no Venetian canals. His dream tosses him straight into her room, still messy with snack plates, dropped lipstick, screwed up revision about 'the liver'; scrawled words – 'Alone along the icy street', and a sock with hearts. Her lilac, starry pyjamas lie in a heap on the floor. Underneath the trousers, he finds her hair straighteners, cold but still plugged in. When he picks them up, they're suddenly hot, oozing with blood, which spreads like a flood rising from the drains, till it's up to his ankles. He shrieks when he catches sight of her face, which floats, unfocused, in the wavy mirror, mouths 'Dad! Dad!' Then she's gone.

*The nightmare will not be pushed under. In the morning, Matthew finds that Rowan has not returned to her bedroom. The creatures on her walls swim a riddle. When he finally falls asleep the next night, Matthew finds himself called to the well at top of the Green…*

*Ratsastaa arvoituksen selässä*

Ne astuvat yli tuhkakuppien, maalattujen auringonnousujen.

Siennassa hän näki sellaisen aaltoilevan lipussa
kirkonovea korkeampana

Kerran hän näki vilahdukselta kaaren hipovan aallonharjaa
huimaava pudotus kalliolta Cornwallissa.

Ne ilakoivat kirjankansissa, näytönsäästäjissä.

Hänen veljensä sanoi: näemme ne läpi
kurakaonsinen, altaissa kuvatut.

Ne sukeltava lasin läpi, laskeutuvat kylpyhuoneiden matoille.

Ne tönivät nenillä lapsia, pian kuolevia
kehdottavat ennen unta

*To ride on the back of a riddle*

They leap across ashtrays, painted sunsets.

In Siena, he saw one ripple on a flag
waved higher than a church door.

Once, he glimpsed a curve nudge tufts of sea
a dizzy drop from a Cornish cliff.

They frisk on book covers, screen savers.

His brother said we watch them through
curaçao blue, filmed in pools.

They dive through glass, land on bathmats.

They nuzzle children soon to die,
lullaby them before sleep.

*Kun kuu roihuaa valkoisena*
    *Elizabeth Bishopin mukaan*

Hän herää kun alkaa valjeta.
sininen delfiini puhuu:
Mene veteen,
ota viisipiikkinen harava.
Hän ei näe puhujaa, vaan kuulee äänen,
se kuulostaa vanhalta naiselta,
ikkunan alla ärhentelevältä.
Hän heittää peiton pois,
hyppää eilisiin housuihin,
pujahtaa kenkiin, hakee haravan.

Delfiini huokaisee ylhäällä,
Kukkula tömähtelee, kun hän juoksee.
Hän potkii purkkeja ja lasinsirpaleita.
Seljat narisevat.
Alkaa sataa.
Hän haravoi ja haravoi,
näykkii maata
kynsillään,
hieroo otsaansa.
Hänen hiuksensa haisevat mudalle.
Kädet piikeistä punaiset.
Sitten hän löytää sen,
Underwater Love –t-paita,
mutta jokea ei ole, ei merta.

Hän nostaa esiin lenkkitossun.
Delfiini huokaisee taas.
Hän raivaa tieltään horsmaa,
taistelee nokkosia vastaan, haavoittaa kätensä
karhuvatukoissa ja karkeassa hiekassa,
näkee kaivon kivireunan
ja mytyn kangasta.

Tyttö on neljäs, jonka hän on nähnyt:
Sitan isä huolellisesti maalattu,
hoikka nainen sariin kääritty
liikenteejakajalla Dhakassa,
koulupoika bussin renkaan alla.

*When the moon burns white*
　　*After Elizabeth Bishop*

He gets up at light.
A blue dolphin speaks:
'Go to the water.
Bring a rake with five prongs.'
He can't see her but she grunts
like an old woman
beneath his window.
He pulls on yesterday's trousers,
slides into shoes, fetches the rake.

The dolphin sighs from higher up.
The hill thuds as he runs.
He kicks cans and broken glass.
The elder trees creak.
It begins to rain.
He rakes and rakes,
picks at the ground
with his fingernails,

rubs his forehead.
His hair smells of mud.
His hands are stung red.
Then he finds the t-shirt:
'Underwater Love'.
No river, no sea.

He drags out her trainer.
The dolphin sighs again.
He pulls aside willow herb,
fights nettles, bloodies his hands
with brambles and grit.
He spots the stone edge of a well,
sees a crumple of cloth.

She's the fourth he's ever seen:
Sita's father carefully painted;
a thin woman in a sari
on a traffic island in Dhaka;
the schoolboy under the tyre of a bus.
This one is his sweetheart.
She never let him tell her that.

Mutta tämä on hänen kullannuppunsa,
vaikkei tyttö koskaan antanut sitä kertoa.

Sitten juoksemista, huuto, yksi puhelu.
Siniset valot, ambulanssi,
kuvaelma univormuja,
verkkainen nostaminen,
nauha Greenin ympärillä.

Seuraavan kerran hän näkee tyttönsä pöytälaatikossa
ja tietää, ettei se ole hän,
että tyttö on sukeltanut delfiinin kanssa,
että hänen täytyy seurata.

### Halkaista lasinen jyvä

*Viikko Rowanin kuoleman jälkeen: ei mahdollisuutta hautajaisiin. Helvetti ennen surua, kun järkytys on tuore eikä ole aikaa ajatella, ei valmiutta itkeä.*

*Puolessa välissä elämänsä tarinaa, Matthew astuu veteen etsimään tytärtään. Tyttö on kuusitoista. Hän on kuollut. Hän on elossa. Matthew ei voi menettää häntä. Muut isät menettävät tyttäriä, muut tyttäret isiä.*

*Matthew putoaa pimeään. Tämä matka: hän vapisee ajatellessaan sitä. Toiset eivät halua tätä tarinaa kerrottavan. He jättäisivät sen maan alle.*

Then it's all running, scream, phone call.
Blue lights, the ambulance,
a tableau of uniforms,
slow lifting,
tape round the Green.

Next time he sees her, she's in a drawer:
he knows it's not her.
She's dived with the dolphin:
he knows he must go.

## Splitting the glassy grain

*A week after Rowan's death: no chance of a funeral. The limbo before mourning, when the shock's fresh and there's no time to think.*

*Halfway through the story of his life, Matthew enters water to search for his daughter. She is sixteen. She is dead. She is alive. He cannot lose her. Other fathers lose daughters, other daughters lose fathers.*

*Matthew drops into darkness. This journey: he shudders when he thinks of it. Others would like this tale not to be told. They would like to leave it underground.*

*Syöksy*

Viikko kulunut, hän sulkee mielestään tyttärensä
　　　　lempikappaleen,
kaataa mustaa kahvia tiskialtaaseen.

"Mene alas, halkeamien läpi."

Hän pakkaa huilunsa, ruokaa,
vedenpitävän taskulampun, purukumia,
kävelee Greenin huipulle,
hän riisuu kengät ja sukat,
pudottaa kiven, kuulee molskahduksen.
Aika. Hän hyppää, lyö olkapäänsä
kaivon reunaan, naarmuttaa ihonsa.

Hän iskeytyy veteen, vajoaa alas.
Mustelmat tulevat myöhemmin.
Hän ui kuin rukous,
työntää sivuilleen kylmää,
pidättää hengitystä, sulkee silmät.

Hän ponnahtaa pintaan, haukkoo ilmaa.
Katsoo tippukiviä pitkin ylös.
Mädäntyneiden lehtien maiskahdukset
valkoisten varpaitten välissä.

Hänen katseensa lakaisee mutaa.
Sitten huojuva möykky puolen luolaa edempänä.
Kalpea, niin kuin kuollut sammakko
jonka hän löysi muovipeitteen alta
puita pinotessaan.
Pikemminkin manaatti kuin defliini,
möykky limalevää,
ehkä kolmen metrin pituinen.
Ja ne samat huokaukset.

Se ui, räpyläinen puunrunko.
Hän kahlaa vyötärönsyvään, seuraa.

*Plunge*

One week gone, he shuts out her favourite tune,
pours black coffee down the sink.

'Go down, through the cracks.'

That night he packs his flute, torch, gum,
walks to the top of the Green,
takes off shoes and socks,
drops a stone, hears the splash far down.
Time. He jumps, catching his shoulder
on the well's rim, scraping skin.

He hits water, goes under.
Bruises will come later.
He swims on like a prayer,
shoves aside cold,
holds breath, shuts eyes.

He breaks water, gulps for air,
looks up at stalactites.
There's a squelch of slurry
between his white toes.

His eyes sweep the slick.
Then a lump heaves
half the cave away,
bleached, like the dead frog
he found under plastic sheet
when he stacked the logs.
More manatee than dolphin,
a lumber of slime algae
three metres long.
The same sighs as before.

She swims, a finned tree trunk.
He wades waist deep, follows.

*Mikä jäi kesken*

*Hän avaa pienen arkun
jossa on kolme ruumiinosaa.
Ne lepäävät sinisellä sametilla.*

Kukka hopeakoskettimilla
on johtolanka kosteisiin paikkoihin,
sormien poissaolo,
kiinni ommeltu suu, sydän
lukittuna toiseen rasiaan.

Hahlotettuna yhteen, kolme osaa
tulee yhdeksi, jäinen putkilo
sykkii hänen kädessään, yhä
soitin johon hän rakasti
laulaa, sokeltaa ja livertää.

Kevyempi kuin hän muisti,
kuin ontto luu,
suomalaisen polkan askelet,

Papagenon linnunlaulu
höyheniselle Papagenalleen.

Hän puhaltaa hengästyneen nuotin,
tietää kadottaneensa heiveröisen sointinsa –
kaislikon synkän joen äärellä,
urut Fen – kirkossa –
kynttilänliekin puhalluksen.

Skaala ei tuo lohtua:
ääni on ohut, kuin vaimeneva teepannu
Rayburn –liedellä lapsena:
keittiövihellys, sopimaton
Debussyn kuvitelemalle Panille.

Hän soittaa matalan B:n
josta huilistit unelmoivat,
sitten säkeen, sen mitä hän muistaa
Panhuilusta, mutta se riittää
pysäyttämään korppikotkat.

*Picking up*

*He opens a miniature black coffin
which contains three body parts.
They rest on a bed of blue velvet.*

Bloom on the silver keys
is a clue to damp places,
an absence of fingers,
a mouth sewn shut, a heart
locked in another case.

Slotted together, three parts
become one, an icy tube
pulsing in his hands, still
the instrument he loved
to sing into, slur and trill.

Lighter than he remembers,
like a hollowed bone,
the steps of a Finnish Polka,
the birdsong of Papageno
for his feathered Papagena.

He stutters one breathy note,
knows he's lost his reedy tone –
bulrushes by a gloomy river,
a pipe organ in a Fen church –
to a feeble candle blow.

There's no comfort in the scale:
it's a thin sound, like a dying kettle
from his Rayburn childhood:
a kitchen whistle, unsuited
to Debussy's imagined Pan.

He tongues the B flat
which all flute players dream,
then a phrase, all he remembers
of 'Syrinx', but enough
to stop the vultures.

*On vielä paljon kirjoittamatta ja lukematta. Matthew'n huilu herättää hänen tyttärensä varjoisaan elämään. Kesällä hän katoaa toistuvasti näköpiiristä johdattaessaan Matthewia ali Leedsin, Goolen, Hullin, poikki Pohjanmeren ja ali Ruotsin aina Vaasan kaduille, jossa hän katoaa taas. Hän samoaa syksyn lyheneviä päiviä keskellä metsiä ja Pohjanmaan kohoavia saaria, kunnes löytää hänet viimeisen kerran.*

*There are many more writings yet to be written and yet to be read. Matthew's flute brings his daughter to shadowy life. Throughout the summer, she constantly disappears from his sight as she leads him under Leeds, Goole, Hull, across the North Sea and beneath Sweden to the streets of Vaasa, where he loses her once more. During the shortening days of autumn, he searches among the forests and rising islands of Ostrobothnia, until he finds her for the last time.*

*Adam on Marko*

So many times I've looked through the ice to see Marko standing underwater.

He looks up, offers me troll bones, a photograph of his mother's hair and the crackling candle in his hands. He takes one step and, like a prophet, delivers a perfect English saying, ancient and modern:

> *There are people in us without names, birthdays.*

After twelve more steps, he arrives where broken ice floats on brackish water, emerges and shakes my hand with his cold fingers. His tallness gently dominates the lake's shore. He rubs fish scales from his forearms, elucidates the connection between Dostoyevsky and Traci Lords in his carefully beautiful English.

My pleasure in Marko's work is sensuous and enviously unbelieving. How can this Finn write in such tantalising English, packed with precise observation and ideas? Marko wrote 'Thirteen Steps Underwater' in English and then translated his own work into Finnish. Or did he? Perhaps, when he's writing, both languages somehow co-exist, leading to an inventive, newly minted prose. But to this Englishman, his writing seems very Finnish: it smells of students' dark attic rooms, twisted creatures slithering in the endless forest and alchemy which tries to conjure up gold women during the endless winter.

Marko knows *The Kalevala* as a lugubrious friend. He places names from the epic as titles for each 'step underwater', giving himself permission to create lucid frames of biography, dream and family history. He wears the black coat of isolation and small town-ness which gives rise to a bleak, detailed imagination rooted in the everyday. He's an expert on Blake's poetry and knows about heavy metal bands. He smiles, makes jokes and sometimes talks about old gods.

# Thirteen Steps Underwater

# Kolmetoista askelta veden alla

Marko Hautala

*1.*

**Gap** [´gæp]: *lovi*

Junat lumoavat. Muistot rakastavat raiteiden rytmiä, välkkyvää pimeyttä paikkojen välissä. Ne ajelehtivat näkökenttään, kolhitun vaunun keinunta kutsuu esiin.

Vaan vettä kauemmas ei voi muistaa. Monet ovat yrittäneet, pienet ja suuret. Juopot, sivilisaatiot. Ikkuna on musta. Vain pakenevat vesipisarat.

Varo pudotusta, ääni sanoo.

Hydraulinen sihahdus. Sateessa löyhkää ruoste.

Pudottaudun.

*1.*

**Lovi** [LDVI]: *gap*, (archaic) *trance*

Trains put me in a trance. Memories love the rhythm of the tracks, the flickering darkness between this place and that. They drift to view, charmed by the sway of the battered carriage.

But you can't remember further than water. Many have tried, great and small, drunks, civilisations. The window is black but for the trickles of water, escaping.

Mind the gap, the voice says.

Hydraulic hiss. The rain smells of rust.

I plunge.

*2.*

**She Who Drowns Forever** [ˈʃiː ˈhuː ˈdraʊns fəˈrevə]: *Aino*

Yhdeksänvuotiaana äitini melkein hukkui.

Kymmenen vuotta myöhemmin synnyin, ja hän yritti opettaa minut pelkäämään nestemäisiä asioita kuten vettä, moniselitteisiä kirjoja ja alkoholia. Siten upotti minut niihin.

Synnyin kesäkuussa. Isoäitini oli vielä elossa ja ehkä auringonpaiste sai hänet unohtamaan hermostuneet talvet, sturmovikkien jyrinän ja sen kun hän juoksi muiden lasten kanssa ulos, makasi hangessa valkoisen lakanan alla ja lumi suli hätääntyneiden sydämenlyöntien alla. Se kesäkuu oli ennätyskuuma, ja ehkä hän hymyili, kuuli kärpäsen pörinän ikkunaa vasten. Ehkä hän joi vettä ja katsoi puita ulkona ja ajatteli: kukaan ei ikinä kuole.

Silloin kesäkuussa äitini oli yhdeksäntoista ja piteli minua ensimmäistä kertaa siinä pikkukaupungissa, petollisten hiekkasärkkien ja tekojärvien piirittämässä, lasten nauru, läiskähdys kun he hyppäävät veteen, kupliva hiljaisuus. Minä, juuri vedestä tullut. He, haastavat toisiaan vapisevin äänin, kilpailevat kuka pidättää hengitystä kauimmin, yksi heistä hukkuu.

*Ne jotka olivat ja menivät ennen meitä.*

Näen kelluvat hiukset ja tytön, joka pidättää hengitystä 5. kesäkuuta 1973.

*Muuttuvat veden aaveiksi, kun muistamme heidät.*

En koskaan tavannut häntä, en tiedä elääkö hän.

*Epävarmoja muistoja kuin haamukipuja.*

Elikö koskaan. Silti muistan auringon välkkeen hiuksilla.

*Meissä on ihmisiä ilman nimiä, syntymäpäiviä.*

Käteni näyttää toiselta heti, kun painan sen pinnan alle, ja taas hän on siellä, kyyhöttää veden alla, uneksii syntymästä, hukkuu.

## 2.

**Aino** [ɑɪnɒ]: *she who drowns forever*

My mother almost drowned at the age of nine.

Ten years later I was born, and she tried to imprint in me a fear of liquid substances such as water, ambiguous books and alcohol. By doing that, she submerged me in them

I was born in June. My grandmother was still alive and perhaps the sunshine made her oblivious of the nervous winters, the roar of Russian Sturmoviks and how she ran outside with the other children, how she hid under a white sheet and lay still, snow melting away under her panicky heartbeat. That June, the hottest ever, she probably smiled and heard a fly buzzing against a window. Perhaps she drank water, saw the trees outside and thought, no one ever dies.

That June my mother was nineteen and she held me for the first time in that small town surrounded by treacherous sandbanks and reservoirs, children laughing, jumping into the water with a splash followed by the bubbling silence. Me, just emerged from water. Them, daring each other in shaky voices, competing who could hold their breath the longest, one of them drowning.

*Those who were and went before us.*

I see a young girl with floating hair holding her breath on the 5th of June 1973.

*Become ghosts in the water when remembered.*

I've never met her, don't know if she's still alive.

*Uncertain memories like phantom limbs.*

If she ever was. Still I remember the flicker of the waves on her hair.

*There are people in us without names or birthdays.*

My hand looks different the moment I put it below the surface, and again she is there, curled up underwater, dreaming of birth, dying.

*3.*

**Water-Breathers** [ˈwɔːtə ˈbriːðəs]: *hiidet*

Pitkiä päiviä meren äärellä. Aaltojen ääni ja kaislojen tuoksu yhdistyvät yhdeksi aistimukseksi, sen kaiku kutittaa korvia ja sieraimia ennen nukahtamista. Neuvostojohtajat hymyilevät Helsingissä. Televisiossa hävittäjät melkein koskettavat. Neljä vuodenaikaa ja ydintalvi tekee viisi. Mutta aamu tulee aina, välinpitämättömänä, ennalta arvattavana, niin kuin aallot. Vesi muuttuu vihreästä kullanruskeaksi, kirkkaasta sameaksi ja takaisin.

Usein kuvittelin, että ne katsovat veden läpi. Puolikuolleet, puolijumalat. Liikkeet mudan ja merilevän hidastamat. Ne huojuvat aaltojen tahdissa. Silmät suurina, lasinharmaina, täynnä vedenhengittäjien julmaa viisautta.

Muistan ukkoskesät. Siilot. Ydinkärjet. Molskahdukset. Naurun. Ja kun ranta jäi liian kauas, kylmät sormet varpaissani.

*4.*

**The Grove of Death** [ˈðə ˈɡrəʊv ˈəv ˈdeθ]: *Tuonen lehto*

On paikkoja, joissa kuolema viipyy.

Vuosisatoja epätoivoiset naiset synnyttivät tällä rannalla, hukuttivat äpäränsä järveen. Eikä ihme oikeastaan, koivut täällä näyttävät viisailta, välinpitämättömiltä. Mutta on liian helppoa kuvitella se kaikuva tyyni juuri ennen auringonlaskua. Pienet sormet avautuvat hitaasti. Päästävät veden sisään.

Juuri kun nuo turhat, kolkot kuolemat voi nähdä liian paljaina, vailla sanoja tai tarkoitusta, käärme luikertaa veteen, ui.

Vesi. Äkkiä se on ääretön. Kuunkylmä sormissani, kun nostan ylös pienen luun.

## 3.

**Hiidet** [hiːdet]: *water-breathers*

Long days by the sea. Sound of the waves and smell of the reeds becoming a single sensation, its echo tickling our ears and nostrils even at night, before falling asleep. Soviet leaders smiling in Helsinki. Fighter planes almost touching on TV. The four seasons plus nuclear winter makes five. But the morning always comes, impassive and predictable, like the waves. Water numbs our words, dims the sun. Water, shifting from green to golden brown, from clear to murky and back.

I often imagined creatures looking through. Half dead, half gods. Movements slowed by the mud and tender stranglehold of the seaweed. They sway in time with the waves. Eyes wide, glass-grey, and full of the cruel wisdom of those who breathe liquid.

I remember those thundery summers. Silos. Warheads. Splashes. Laughter. And when the shore got too far, cold fingertips on my toes.

## 4.

**Tuonen lehto** [tuɒnen lehtɒ]: *the grove of death*

There are places where death lingers.

For centuries, desperate women gave birth on this shore, drowned their bastards in the lake. It's understandable in its way; the birches here seem wise, disinterested. But it's too easy to imagine. The echoing calm just after the sunset. Small fingers opening slowly. Giving in to water.

Just when the image of those futile, dreary deaths becomes too plain, empty of words or meaning, a snake enters the water, swims.

Water. It is limitless, suddenly. Cold on my fingertips like a moon as I, stupefied and not believing, lift up a small bone.

## 5.

**Mistress of the North** [ˈmɪstrɪs ˈəv ˈð ˈnɔːθ]:
*Louhi*

Kun vedet jäätyvät, puut pidättävät henkeään.

Aurinko on heikko ja hidas, ryömii
kuusenlatvoja hipoen. Ikkunat sumenevat
pakkasesta, kalpeasta, sinisestä, loputtomasta.
Kaamoksen ennuste: aistit kääntyvät sisäänpäin,
levittävät sormensa, tunnustelevat tietään
pimeässä.

(Kohenna tulta. Kuuntele.)

Jos löydät kolmituumaisen halkeaman jäässä
ja seuraat sitä pohjoiseen, jos kävelet läpi
lumipyörteiden kuin toisten maailmojen
verhojen, löydät siivekkään vanhan naisen.
Sanoista vapisevan. Tuulen mykistämän.
Menetyksestä raskaan. Melkein uskon sen.

## 6.

**The Mute Creatures of the Cold** [ˈðə ˈmjuːt ˈkriːtʃəs ˈəv ˈðə ˈkəʊld]: *manalaiset*

Marraskuun lopun pimeys ei ole puute. Se ei vain
ole ihmisestä. Se haisee jumalilta.

5.

**Louhi**: [lɒuhɪ]: *mistress of the North*

When the waters freeze, the trees hold their breath.

The sun is weak and slow, barely able to reach the spruce tops. The window dims with frost, pale and blue and endless. A prognosis of *kaamos*: the senses turn inwards, spread their fingers inside, feel their way in the dark.

(Poke the fire. Listen.)

If you find a three-inch crack in the ice and follow it up north, walk through the whirls of snow like curtains to other worlds, you'll find an old woman with wings. Shivering with words. Muted by the wind. Pregnant with loss. I've never been this close to believing.

6.

**Manalaiset** [mʌnʌlɪset]: *the mute creatures of the cold*

The darkness in late November is not a lack. It just isn't human. It smells of gods.

## 7.

**The Peasant With a Mitre** [ˈðə ˈpeznt ˈwið ə ˈmaɪtə]: *Lalli*

Sarvet, kärsät, hampaat, hännät, sorkat, pallosilmät.

Tässä kirkossa, maan vanhimmassa, voi nähdä hengityksensä ja kuulla yskähdykset kymmenkertaisena. Aiheuttaa synnintuntoa ja saa välittämään sen seuraavalle sukupolvelle. Katson haalistuneita seinämaalauksia, kunnes niskaan sattuu, olen huolissani siitä, miten hengitys kuolee juuri ennen kuin saavuttaa apostolit. On jouluaamu ja saarna on sama, ilma ei. Kynttilät räiskähtelevät, ärtyneenä kylmästä.

Kesken saarnan, tylsistyneenä ja nuhaisena, ajattelen Lallin tarinaa.

Tarina kääntyy mumisevaksi evankeliumiksi, riitasointuiseksi joululauluksi, kuva josta pitäisi tehdä alttaritaulu. Yksinäinen talonpoika jäällä, pitelee päätään ja hiippaa, joka tippuu verta. Uskontunnustuksemme hukassa lumimyrskyssä. Murhaaja kävelee vetten päällä. Sarvet, kärsät, hampaat. Niin ne kasvatetaan.

Mutta koska heidän Lallinsa on maalattu tarpeettoman mykäksi, lukutaidottomaksi ja pukinsorkkaiseksi, hahmottelen omani puhuvan näin ennen kuin piispa menettää päänsä:

*Rakas Henrik,*

*Uskonnot ovat silmiä, sinun omasi on likinäköinen. Näkee yhden jumalan siellä, missä on monta.*

Tsop.

Ei kovin tyylikästä sekään, mutta kynttilät näyttävät pitävän. Rätisevät liekit tyyntyvät, venyvät. Niiden kulta leviää kirkon seinille ja niiden läpi ja takaperin vuosisatoja, Köyliön jäälle ja piispa Henrikin likinäköisiin silmiin. Lumihiutaleet sulavat hänen laajeneviin pupilleihinsa, hänen huulensa sinertyvät rukoukseen, veri leviää hitaasti, sädekehä jäällä.

Saarna oli kristuslapsesta, joka hymyili ja heilutti käsiään tietäjille. Tietämättään pyyhki maailmoja.

# 7.

**Lalli** [lʌllɪ]: *the peasant with a mitre*

Horns, snouts, fangs, tails, hooves, bulging eyes. A ragged gallery of old gods.

In this church, one of the oldest in the country, you can see your breath and hear your every cough tenfold. Makes you feel contrition and pass it down the generations. I look up at the bleached paintings until my neck hurts, worried by the way my breath dies just before reaching the apostles. It's Christmas morning and the reading is the same but the air is not. The candles crackle, vexed by cold.

Mid-sermon, bored and having the sniffles, I come to think of the story of Lalli, the pagan peasant who killed Bishop Henrik. It was on the ice of Lake Köyliö almost a thousand years ago.

Henrik came to Lalli's house when he was away, the story goes. He ate and drank and, being the honest Christian that he was, paid the mistress of the house for everything. But when Henrik left and Lalli returned, the wife got all cunning for no apparent reason and lied to her husband. A bishop paid a visit, she said, and ate and drank but did not pay a single dime. Lalli got furious, went after the man of God, killed him with an axe.

As always with these stories, there's a good Christian lesson in it: in a flush of victory, Lalli tried on the slaughtered bishop's mitre and it got stuck on his head. Terrified, he tore it off by force, and his scalp with it.

That story translates into a mumbling gospel, sings a dissonant carol, an image worthy of an altarpiece. A lonely peasant stumbling on the ice of Lake Köyliö, holding his head and a mitre dripping with blood. Our creed lost in a snowstorm. A murderer walking on water. Horns, snouts, fangs. That's how they're grown.

But as their Lalli has been painted unjustly dumb, illiterate and cloven-hoofed, I draft my version so before beheading the priest:

*Dear Henrik,*
*Religions are eyes. Yours is short-sighted. Seeing one god where there's many.*

Chop.

Not too elegant either, but the candles seem

8.

**The Native Land** [ðə neɪtɪv lænd]: *isänmaa*

Tätä maata ei ole nimetty. Sen linnut kömpelöitä symboleja. Järvet eivät inspiroi lauluja.

Historia ei tapahtunut täällä. Uskonnot eivät löytäneet uskojia. Tiedemiehiä ei kiinnostanut.

Koskaan ei sotilas, halvaantunut ja vereen tukehtuva, katsonut lumihiutaleiden lipumista puidenlatvojen välistä. Koskaan ei esi-isä palvonut karhunkalloa koivujen katveessa. Lehdet kasvavat ja kuihtuvat ilman tunnustusta, luokitusta. Eikä järven pohja ole ekosysteemi, vaan pantomiimi märkiä silmiä, pieniä suita mykässä rukouksessa.

Ja kun kaikki makaa näin hiljaa, koskemattoman lumen vaimentamana, havahdun varastettu hiilenpala kädessäni ja alan hahmotella taas.

pleased. Their crackling flames subside, grow longer. Their golden calm spreads on the walls of the church and through them and back the centuries to Lake Köyliö, on dying bishop Henrik's myopic little eyes. Snowflakes disappear into his dilating pupils, his lips turn blue but still in prayer, blood spreads slowly, a halo on the ice.

The sermon was about the infant Christ, smiling and waving his hands to the Magi. Unknowingly wiping out worlds.

*8.*

**Isänmaa** [ɪsænmɑː]: *the native land*

This land has not been named. Its birds make bad symbols. Its lakes inspire no hymns.

History did not happen here. Religions found no believers. Scientists took no interest.

A soldier, paralysed and choking on blood, never did look at snowflakes floating down between the trees. An ancestor never worshipped a bearskull among the birches. Their leaves grow and wither unsung, unclassified. And the bottom of the lake is not an ecosystem but a pantomime of watery eyes, small mouths in mute prayer.

And when all things lie silent, muzzled by untouched snow, I wake up with a stolen piece of coal in my hand and start drafting anew.

## 9.

**The Smith** [ðə smɪθ]: *Ilmarinen*

Hän näki juuri peikon viilettävän pihan poikki.

*Tiedän että valo on petollinen*, hän sanoo, *mutta minä näin*. Hän hieroo tahraisia käsiään ja pälyilee huonetta. Hän kuiskaa:

*Joka aamu sulatan lunta pannussa ja kaadan kahviin Stolishnajaa. Luen ääneen* Aurora Consurgensia. *Pidän kirjaa tähtien asennosta ja paskani väristä. Pohdiskelen veritas efficaciaen sävyjä. Piirrän kuvia kultaisesta naisesta ja poltan ne kamiinassa. Jäädytän spermaani logos spermatikosin kuviksi. Laitan kattilaan kultaa, sulatan sen saunan tulipesässä, annan sen kovettua, kauhistelen epäsikiötä, sulatan taas häpeän vimmalla.*

Prosessi on herkkä, monimutkainen ja turhauttava. Hän työskentelee ja työskentelee, aamuisin nöyrän huolellisesti, iltaisin kömpelönä suuruudenhulluudesta. Metsä kaikuu paukahduksista, ulvonnasta, sairaankeltaisen valon välähdyksistä. Sudet laahustavat puiden välissä, nuuhkivat ja tuhahtelevat, pelon ja uteliaisuuden umpikujassa. Hän sanoo:

*Joskus pöllöt lepattavat pois kuin nauru. Joskus sudet kusevat väkeviä viestejä lumipenkkaan. Vastaan vapisevin keltaisin kirjaimin, pyydän pientä kunnioituksen pisaraa. Sillä työ on kirous, jota eläin tai lintu ei voi ymmärtää.*

Kuu paisuu, se häilyy ilta illalta suurempana, kuolleiden meriensä ruhjoma. Saunan ikkunat huurtuvat ja hohtavat pimeässä, kuin joku kiduttaisi aurinkoa sen rähjäisten lautojen takana. Metsässä sudet ja sanat kiertävät toisiaan, haistavat verta. Sisällä, savussa ja liassa ja kuumuudessa, kulta sihisee ja kuplii. Hänen hirviönsä yrittää puhua.

Sulaa, kovaa, sulaa taas.

Sulaa, kovaa, sulaa. Ja hän sanoo:

*Jossakin hajoamisen takana, tylsän vääjäämättömyyden ja äkkinäisen raivon takana, hahmo saa muotonsa. Silmät räpyttelevät, nytkähtelevä symmetria, vaappuva tasapaino.*

Yö toisensa jälkeen, unenpuutteen ja Stolishnajan voimalla, hän puhuu kultaisesta naisesta, joka kävelee läpi savun. Askeleiden alla sulavasta lumesta, silmistä jotka avautuvat kuin unessa.

# 9.

**Ilmarinen** [ɪlmʌrɪnen]: *the smith and his al khemeia*

He just saw a troll scurry across the yard.

I know the light is unreliable, he says, but I saw. He rubs his stained hands and browses the room. He whispers:

Every morning, I melt snow in the coffeepot and pour Stolichnaya in the coffee. I read Aurora Consurgens aloud. I keep a notebook on the positions of the stars and colour of my excrement. I meditate on the veritas efficaciae. I draw pictures of a golden woman and burn them in the stove. I freeze my semen in the image of the logos spermatikos. I put gold in my cauldron, melt it on the sauna stove, let it congeal, shudder at the monster, then melt it again in an embarrassed haste.

The process is fragile, complicated and frustrating. He works and works, with humble preciseness in the mornings and clumsy megalomania in the evenings. The forests echo with the bangs and howls and flashes of sickly yellow light. Wolves slouch between the trees, sniffing and snorting, trapped in a stalemate of fear and curiosity. He says:

Sometimes the owls flap away like laughter. Sometimes the wolves piss pungent messages in the snow bank. I answer in my shaky yellow letters, asking for a tiny drop of respect. Because the work is a curse in ways no bird or beast could begin to understand.

The moon swells, looms bigger every night, bruised by its dead oceans. The sauna windows steam and glow in the night as if someone was torturing the sun behind the creaky boards. In the forest, wolves and words circle around, chasing each other, smelling blood. Inside, in the smoke and dirt and heat, gold sputters and bubbles. His monster trying to speak.

Melt, congeal, melt again in haste.

Melt, congeal, melt. And he says:

Somewhere beneath the mindless process of decay, between dull necessity and sudden fury, a form pulls through. Eyes blinking, symmetry twitches, a hovering balance.

And night after night, fuelled by Stolichnaya and insomnia, he speaks of a golden woman emerging through the smoke, of snow hissing away under her footsteps, of eyes opening like in sleep.

*10.*

**The Severed Son** [ðə sevəːd ˊsʌn]: *Lemminkäinen*

Joka kevät hullu nainen ajelehtii joen jäälle kuin savu. Sormet pyyhkivät pois hennon lumen, jään kosketus valkean nenän päähän saa hänet värähtämään, kun hän katsoo läpi jäätyneiden oksien ja kuplien ja hyönteisten tähtikuvion.

Hän näkee pojan siellä pimeässä.

Vain sameina palasina, jotka keinuvat mudan ja planktonin ja humusvirtojen tahdissa kuin vedenalaisessa sumussa. Silmäkuopat vielä tyhjät, alaleuka kateissa. Sidekalvot leijuvat hitaassa itkuvirressä rikottujen luiden yllä.

Hänen hengityksensä höyryää kylmässä.

*Rakennan sinut.*

Jos on kärsivällisyyttä ja tupakkaa istua päiviltä tuntuvan ajan, voi muutoksen haistaa. Vesi elpyy. Jää murtuu. Luut kääntyvät kuin huokaukset pimeässä.

10.

**Lemminkäinen** [lemmınkæınen]: *the severed son*

Every spring, a madwoman drifts like smoke into the middle of the river. Her fingers wipe away the fine cover of snow, she shudders from the touch of ice against her pointy white nose as she looks through the frozen constellations of twigs and bubbles and insects.

And she sees him in the darkness below.

Only as blurred fragments, cradled by mud and plankton and humic currents like coal dust or underwater fog. His eye sockets are still empty, his lower jaw is missing. Membranes floating in slow lamentation above the scattered bones.

Her breath steams in the cold.

*I will build you.*

If you have enough patience and cigarettes to sit still for what feels like days, you can smell the change. The water quickens. Ice cracks. Bones turn like moans in the black.

*11.*

**The Lost Spring** [lɒst sprɪŋ]: *kadonnut kevät*

Se miten lumi heijastaa valoa kevään ensimmäisenä päivänä muistuttaa siitä, kun olit vielä elossa ja vedimme kännit ja keskustelimme Freudista, Dostojevskista ja Traci Lordsista ja lopulta imppasimme liimaa, koska emme olleet tehneet sitä ja kotimatkalla kaaduin selälleni keskelle jalkapallokenttää ja katsoin lumihiutaleiden syöksähtelyä ja tajusin, että tyttöystäväni on lesbo, mutten soittanut sille.

Muistot tuntuvat hälyttävän vierailta, kun ne tulevat kutsumatta. Lumihiutaleet kohoavat ja syöksyvät kuin kalat arvaamattomissa kierteissä, pilkkaavat näkökentän rajoja, kun etsit muotoa.

*12.*

**Death** [deθ]: *Tuoni*

Sinä. Yli. Joen. Ystävä.

*11.*

**Kadonnut kevät** [kʌdɒnnut kevæt]: *the lost spring*

The way light reflects from the snow on the first spring day reminds me of the time when you were still alive and we got drunk, discussed Freud, Dostoyevsky and Traci Lords and eventually sniffed glue because we hadn't done it before and on the way home I fell on my back in the middle of a football field and looked at the snowflakes whooshing and realised my girlfriend was gay but did not ring her.

Memories seem alarmingly unfamiliar, when uninvited. Snowflakes rise and fall like fish in unpredictable spins, challenging the corners of your eyes as you look for a pattern.

*12.*

**Tuoni** [tuɒnɪ]: *Death*

You. Across. River. Friend.

*13.*

**The Mother of All Waters** [ðə mʌðə əv ɔːl wɔtəs]:
*veen emonen*

Vaikkakin ehdollistettuja auringonlaskuihin
ja ajatukseen siitä, että hengitämme valjua
huoneilmaa johonkin suhteelliseen valaistumiseen
saakka, olemme vain karkotettuja kaloja,
valmiina hyppäämään takaisin. Eikä kukaan kysy
mielipidettä, kun kehomme päättää viedä meidät
alas kaikki ne sylet.

Ensin löysit valkeita hiuksia kammastasi,
sitten verta vessapaperista. Loppu on puisevaa
radiografiaa.

Poltat edelleen melkein kaksi askia päivässä
ja vihaat kapitalisteja. Mutta yhä useammin
tunnustelet lapsuusmuistoja kuin tarkistaaksesi,
että ne ovat vielä siellä. Joskus yöllä, sanot, heräät
puristaen sänkysi laitoja, peläten että tulva vie
sinut.

Naurat vitsille, jonka kuulit rakennustyömaalla
Tampereella. Yksi niistä jutuista, jotka muistuttavat
että pohjalla on monta tuttua kasvoa. Kalpeaa,
salaperäistä, ei enää tuskissaan.

*Kasvatamme kidukset, uskoimme mitä tahansa.*
*Kasvatamme suomut, vaikka kuinka haluaisimme*
*lentää. Menemme alas, oli mikä oli.*

Mutta kun poimit sytyttimen tupakkahuoneen
lattialta, liikkeittesi hetkellinen määrätietoisuus
lupaa, että opit hengittämään mahdotonta,
kantamaan vetten painon.

Ja miten toivonkaan, että voisin antaa sinulle pienet
kalansilmät ja sen kipua lievittävän ihmetyksen.
Kuin silittäisi epämuodostumaa. Kuin rakastettu
vilkuttaisi vieraassa kaupungissa. Kuin syvämeren
kala, joka säikähtää valokeilaa. Kuin kävelisi veden
alla, auringonlaskut unohtaneena, tyytyväisenä
pimeään.

## 13.

**Veen emonen** [veːn emɒnen]: *the mother of all waters*

Conditioned as we are to sunsets and the thought of breathing flat room air until some relative enlightenment, we are just fish in exile, preparing to jump back. And I'm afraid no one will ask for our opinions when our bodies decide to take us down those fathoms.

First you found white hair in your comb, then blood on your toilet paper. The rest is dull radiography.

You still smoke nearly two packs a day and hate them capitalists. But more and more often you seem to feel for your childhood memories as if to check that they're still there. Sometimes at night, you tell me, you wake up gripping the sides of your bed, afraid to be carried away by a flood.

You laugh at a joke you heard at a building site in Tampere. One of those stories that assure you there are plenty of familiar faces at the bottom, waiting. Pale, sly, silent, not in pain any more.

*We grow gills, no matter what our religion. We grow scales, no matter how much we'd rather be flying. We go down, no matter what.*

But now, as you pick up your lighter from the floor of the smoking room, a fleeting sense of confidence in your movements tells me you will be taught to breathe the unbreathable, to bear the weight of the waters above you.

And I wish I could give you a pair of little fish eyes and that anaesthetic sense of wonder. Like caressing a deformity. Like your loved-one waving to you in a foreign city. Like a deepwater fish startled by a flashlight. Like walking underwater, oblivious to sunsets, content with the dark.

*During the course of the project the writers exchanged many emails. Here's a selection.*

## Carita and Kath

*14 September 2004*
*to Kath from Carita*
Back from Stockholm I found your new texts, which I've perused with great enjoyment. (A lot of drowning though, it seems, in our texts!) I have translated 'In the Queue for Fish', which I really liked for its wry sense of humour (I had some problems with the fish names; 'headless reds' I read as alluding also to politics, correct me; I think I found a rather funny equivalent, in Swedish 'rodingar' which is a fish name but also a nickname for leftwingers; do you want this double sense of meaning?) and 'Working Metal', having lost my mother in 1988 I'm thoroughly familiar with the theme, which I think you handle beautifully.

Among the new ones I got engaged in 'Rowing across shallows', which I've translated today. Sending you the translation so you can get a idea of how it sounds in Swedish. The two above mentioned I've sent to Ralf, so he can give his comments. Quite exciting that it's already next week you're coming here. I'm trying to recover from a very persistent bronchitis, which does tricks with my voice. Hope it functions next week.

*to Carita from Kath*
Sounds good having the double meaning in 'headless reds'. I'm always fascinated by the nuances of translation. Read the Swedish out loud that you've done – I like the sound of it. I wish I had learnt a little Swedish before. Thanks for doing this. 'Working Metal'… everyone always thinks is about my mother – which it isn't (doesn't make any difference). A friend of mine came round one morning a few weeks after her mother had died and told me the story of having to empty her mother's house. I was fascinated because when my mother died she didn't have that much and we had to clear it all out quickly because the council wanted the flat back as soon as possible. I think writing the poem started from feeling envious of my friend for having the luxury of going through her mother's things slowly. Also my mother didn't keep much except photographs and certainly wouldn't have kept balls of string and elastic. It's interesting what impetus drives you to write a poem.

Been feeling a little insecure about this whole Finnish thing. I was hoping to have a lot more work in progress to do with water on the go, but I feel like I've still just got lots of notes, and my domestic situation at the moment is a bit chaotic. Anyway, the way I am looking at it is if I bring enough for about 20 mins/half an hour to read, vaguely to do with water, I doubt whether we are going to read that much, with all the translations, so we have until November to finalise our ten pages. Have I got it right? Looking forward to hearing everybody else's stuff, and I am sure we will all inspire each other.

*5 January 2005*
*to Kath from Carita*
Just to get my thoughts off the tragedy unravelling in Southeast Asia I've been working on the translations of your poems and reading both your and Adam's texts more thoroughly than before. (Why is one always in such a rush with absolutely everything?) And I have really liked everything I've read: your short story , your introduction from May 04(!!!) Answers many of my questions, but I will return with some more for the article I'm planning for *Astra Nova* about you.

I feel so happy and grateful to be on this team and in this project, but my main concern now is that my own text continues to be cumbersomely formless and incomplete. And that fear-inspiring tsunami keeps coming in the way. Anyway I'm hoping you'd find time to send the complementary texts (among others the one of 'swimming in the waters of your childhood').

*to Carita from Kath*
Hi. Thank you for the translations and the lovely 'Reflection' book. I have been lying on the bed reading and immersing myself in the images. New Year I went to Staithes (near Robin Hood's Bay) and we walked on Boulby Cliff , where in one story Beowulf is buried. A car had gone over the cliff the day before and no body had been found. A rainbow arced right across the cliffs and sea. That seemed a good portent for the first day of 2005. We'd watched fireworks on the beach on New Year's Eve. know what you mean about the writing being 'formless and incomplete'. I have begun on the *Interland* work in the last two days and feel I have along way to go – I am floundering a little, but then I figure my contribution will be a hotch potch of different pieces, and nothing is ever perfect. I spent most of the last few days doing my accounts to send off to the accountant so that I don't get fined for late submission. Every year I surround myself with envelopes and receipts and think how it would be much easier if I was tidier and more organised. Today I went the swimming pool for the first time since Christmas Eve. It was full of people who had obviously made New Year's resolutions. By February it will be empty again. The same with the park and joggers …

This tsunami does make you wonder how we can write about water. I had an email a few days before the tsunami, from a friend who lives in Cornwall in the extreme west of England. She'd spoken of how they'd had giant waves along her beach, waves so high the whole village had come out on the beach to witness them, and how awe inspiring they were. Then my sister wrote from the West of Australia and said how sobering it was looking out at the Indian ocean and knowing it was the same ocean where others had experienced the tsunami.

*31 January 2005*
*to Kath from Carita*
Just back from Helsinki, had a wonderful stay: meeting friends, really good theatre (*Spoonface* by Lee Hall, do you know him?), and some really nice exhibitions, but just ghastly weather: snowstorms, icy winds. But just now just here winter behaves well again, just a few grades minus, wish I could go skiing a bit.

*27 February 2005*
*to Kath from Carita*
Here's the translation minus the Kalevala quotes which I will search for later. Also missing is 'The Fish You Didn't See'. But wanted you to get a general feel of how the translation sounds and looks like. I've taken some liberties here; for ex. with the 'trunks' and 'swimmers'. Also with the 'Stinger'. Used it only in the heading, where it looks great because the Swedish word 'stinger' is a verb (present tense) meaning pierce and burn. A medusa is a type of jellyfish, and sounds so dramatic, Greek mythology etc.

*12 February 2005*
*to Carita from Kath*
Hi. Haven't forgotten about you all, just overwhelmed with practical things. Back to thinking about work. I have just edited and cut my stuff. Will leave it for a day and then have a last look. Meantime I intend looking at yours today and tomorrow, and hopefully anyone else's if there is time. Steve and Adam are busy polishing theirs. I work in Bradford tomorrow – doing that once a week and quite enjoying it (teaching short stories). Also been doing my teeth stuff, and have to start preparing for the workshops in Africa. Steve seems quite keen on a Copenhagen trip, let's pursue it, because it is much easier if you have all the stuff in front of you, in case you want to mess round with the order. How's Ralf? Still silent? Don't know if he has sent the stuff to Steve – haven't been in touch with Steve for a couple of weeks. Anyway, we're getting there. As for the magazine, is it all right if I leave off that till I come back from Africa? (12 March.) I will take the novel with me tomorrow to find a post office between here and Bradford (the day after I wrote to you last time there was a big article and lots of publicity about the widespread closure of post offices in the UK. Finger on the pulse hey?)

I am enjoying my room now. It is clean, sunny and bright. I just have to let the chaos around me (boxes in the hall, filing cabinets, furniture I can't lift myself) fall off me and go to yoga and swimming. Anyway, I'll be in touch as soon as I have read through your stuff. I have glanced at it and it looked like good varied work. Hope you're doing fine. I'd better stop or I'll write a novel.

*25 February 2005*
*to Kath from Carita*
The latest version I got from you is dated Feb.17 and I'm following that in my revised translation. But now then: I'm cutting out 'In at the deep end'. Glad that you keep 'October' : it gives a atmosphere of your locality, geographical and mental, somehow. But the 'deep end' stories may be part of an 'other story' – but who am I to say, skipping wildly in time and space as I am in my own piece. I'm fine but also busy; off now to do an interview with two old Korsnäs friends who have been very active in building up the local museum. I have a very new technique – a recording memory stick easy to put over on a CD – so I'm a bit scared. This weekend trying to find some peace to look through your comments to mine and see what I will do with my text. I keep revising it every time I lie on my bed before sleep. Have a good day in Scarborough, love that coast Whitby – Scarborough, all that I know.

*to Carita from Kath*
I am getting totally confused by now. Did the changes show up in the 17 Feb version? If so, then in that version I have cut out 'In at the Deep End ', 'October' and a few other bits. But as I say I wasn't sure about cutting out 'October'. In that version it is cut out. Maybe I should just send my whole revised version again so that you can check that it is the one we are both working from. Shall I? As for your stuff, if you need anything else looked at, feel free to send it. Can look at bits of stuff this week.

Had a great day in Scarborough – went to see an exhibition and a talk by a Dutch artist – Marielle Harlenson or something like that – the exhibition is called 'Uncanny Tales' – based on fairy tales and myths, with some Paula Rego – don't know if you know her work. Wild and windy on the beach – took tea in a milk bar on the front and bought sugar teeth to inspire us in our teeth project. I'm writing some dark tales.

Have to start really getting my head down about Malawi. I will be away 4 – 13 March so you won't get any answers during that time, but hopefully by the time I get back we will have decided what to do about going on.

Speak to you soon. Hope your illness passes and that you are feeling a little better soon. The tape technique sounds interesting.

*The remainder of this section are all to Kath from Carita*

*21 February 2005*
Back from Helsinki, it was an OK meeting and the evening party meant seeing people I haven't met for ages. The really great thing about these awards is that there are hardly any strings attached …there are no obligations to write reports on what you've done during the year. I find that very satisfying not because I have a need to cheat, but because I think it means that we, the writers, are adult people doing serious work with or without money (the money making it all 'a bit' easier!)

I've always liked Easter, spring in the air and here in Korsnäs always big bonfires on Saturday evening, great chance to get rid of old stuff, and also branches from trees that have been taken down,

*28 February 2005*
I've really enjoyed the work, dreaming about Australia and Stingers and rugby and the moors and reservoirs of Yorkshire.

'Mir y druzba', as some of us used to say.

*18 March 2005*
Still quite severe winter weather – 23 degrees this morning. But it warms up during the day and today there was hardly any wind, so I've spent some time outdoors. We're working with firewood, getting it into the cellar, piling lifting throwing etc…

*April 2005*
…very nice spring weather here now, the winds from the North have subsided. Erik and I try to work in

the garden – in the yard – for an hour or two every day. Next week we'll be painting the house, a 'talko' day meaning friends and neighbours come and assist for free food and good company.

*29 April 2005*
Joyful Walpurgis to you all! It's a big festival here in the North, in Finland mostly meaning greeting spring by choir singing in every park, and otherwise heavy drinking, wild partying. In Sweden bonfires and singing, and getting drunk.

*23 June 2005*
Midsummer greetings.
   In Denmark they call this season St Hans after St Hans Eve and celebrate only the 24/6 evening with bonfires and singing, standing in a circle round the fire, patriotic songs about the beautiful 'Danas Have' garden of Dana. In Finland we have the fire inside of us, i.e. a lot of hard drinking goes on preferably outdoors so you can pass out at Mother Nature's bosom, i.e. ditches and shrubbery and elsewhere.
   … we usually have a nice late meal with new potatoes and gravlax. Young birches by the door, and staying up so you can watch the fairies dance down on the meadows after midnight and watch the sun rise. Weather permitting midsummer's day means taking the first dip in the cold Gulf of Bothnia.

*6 July 2005*
Here we have been struck by a tremendous heatwave: one should be enjoying but up to Monday evening there was such a lot of work to do, so I've been sweating and panting … Jeanette here, she's helping me out with my sadly mismanaged garden, the soil is so dry and dusty, flowers wilting. But the roses are absolutely fantastic this year…
   In the new version the whole piece would have four main parts:
   1) Memories of water
   2) Place descriptions (islands and shores)
   3) Ice stories (but maybe Loquillo has to go – not on ice, but out from the piece)
   4) Back to memories (but tsunami poem goes out)
   … will think of a title, when the heat recedes.

*6 July 2005*
The new version is titled 'Lost and found'.
   It's hothothot here in Korsnäs, have to take a swim and SOON!

*11 July 2005*
Crazy world we live in, hopefully none of your friends were hit in the attacks.

*25 August 2005*
…I'm leaving 'River of Lethe' out, because all effort at amendments seem to take me absolutely nowhere. It just doesn't sound good in English. Also doing hard work on Ran's reign, which I definitely want to keep
   … fantastic weekend in Helsinki meeting my old women's group – after more than 25 years – thirteen of the original 17-strong group turned up. A lot of amazing stories from stormy and less stormy lives. A book is under work (– a journalist

of a younger generation) about women's groups in the seventies (we were mostly Swedish speaking, Finnish girls claimed they had it all! Ha!)

*End August 2005*
I really hope your eye is better now. I just hate having problems with my eyes. You can go on reflecting what's worse for a writer to lose – management of hands, eye-sight etc etc. Ironically enough that it should happen in Copenhagen and during the bicentennial of H C Andersen. You may know that long story of his – I think it's called 'Snow Queen' in English – about Kai who got a 'splinter' in his eye and his vision of the world and people changing drastically.

…sending you a 'final' version. Had to throw out both Lethe and Ran's reign, as I couldn't make them work in English. But I might use them in Swedish in other connections – this whole project has set a lot of writing ideas into motion. One of the really great things about all this…

Cut out a lot of adjectives, and then a new final poem, a bit darker than the Aphrodite one, emerged as late as yesterday … More in accordance with my general mood right now, actually.

*1 September 2005*
I'll keep 'reposed', a bit pompous maybe, queenlike sort of. But it will be fun to see what the PB *[the Poetry Business]* say… what do you think of 'Raking Water' (the PB people will go ballistic, or?) I like it, because that's what we've been doing, raking up things, memories, people, places out of Lethe, the river of forgetting and remembering.

… glorious September weather today, we have a whole day at the museum, rye porridge with lingonberries, stories and spinning in daytime for schoolkids, storytelling by the open fire in the evening, local stories and wonderful music on the old folk instrument called 'Nych elharpa' – sounds like something I have heard in Irish folk music.

*29 September 2005*
The fall has been particularly warm also in Ostrobothnia this year, so I'm still out digging up potatoes, down bulbs and shrubs … Just now I'm in the final efforts of a writing workshop with kids here in Korsnas, theme: talking trees. We're building our very special poetry tree with leaves in all colours featuring their wonderful poems and stories ('tongues in trees').

*3 October 2005*
Gosh, we did miss a whole lot of fun in my student days, I must admit. Just PC marches pro Cuba, anti-US and -Vietnam war etc. Not one BIG BROTHER in sight, me belonging to the (in Finland) cursed and damned New anti-Soviet Left – many a willing comrade would have had me expelled (not to mention worse procedures) for heresy – to Denmark where such views in those days were allowed.

*9 October* **2005**
…marvellously warm and sunny autumn. Plus 14 degrees and sun today … Dag visiting – tied up with his research into beryllium, how it's taken up in various sub-strats. His professor brings various veggies and stuff from his garden to Dag who looks for traces of Beryllium, a shortlived

radioactive substance that comes from cosmic background radiation. Strange and wonderful.

In November I'll rewrite the summer play, into a whole night play. Started writing prose with material from the fifties, too.

*14 October 2005*
For some reason there are mauve skies over Korsnäs this morning; winter lurches round the bend.

*20 October 2005*
Here you can feel winter in the air, darkness closing in over us, but no snow yet, just in Lapland. But we've put winter tyres on the car, just in case. The worst is that black ice on the roads … tomorrow whole day seminar in Vasa on the problems of regional literature – visibility – stuff like that. Ralf and I have 29 minutes to talk about and read from *Interland*, we had a chat yesterday and agreed that this project has been a unique one, meant a lot both to me and Ralf.

*21 November 2005*
… good old friend with whom I wrote my first book from 1975, so we've been toasting in champagne and eating a lot of good food. Also went the Jazz and Poetry at Littfest… Saturday evening listened to a Ukrainian choir singing at Korsnäs church, quite uplifting.

*21 November 2005*
Today it's thirty years since Franco died and I had my first book published in cooperation with Birgitta Boucht … Actually it's also thirty years since Erik and I….etc

Had a long phone talk with Peter Sansom – very good and inspiring – set me working on the texts again.

Finnish winter late this year cannot make up its mind. Frosty days, fantastic weather for walks in the woods, then black and wet again. They say we will soon have 'Danish' winters here up North. I say BLAH!

*Adam and Marko*

*to Marko*
all I've done is make little fiddly suggestions, hopefully in blue.  My only main suggestion is to edit no 12, 'Tuonenvirta' so that it's a little sparer, and sits more easily between the other pieces, but you may want its difference boldly stated.  It's great stuff and I really enjoy it.

*to Adam*
Thank you very much for the comments! Some of them were ones you made already in Yorkshire (*and which I thought I'd already corrected*) so I'm afraid I've got the 100-different-versions-on-two-different-computers problem again. Sorry for that. Anyway, I completely agree with your comments and I'll still work a bit on those parts. But please be prepared for about a thousand questions concerning your text! Looks like it will be THE most challenging translation of the three. Just one example: I can easily (unfortunately) visualise 'blowing goats' and it sounds very classy in Finnish too, but what is 'Rave for the P/F'???
Anyway, I'll write you a lengthy list of all the things I need to check from you after I've finished the first draft.

*to Marko.*
Yes I knew some of the comments I'd already made but your last two texts had a lot of differences (some corrections and some not – though I tried to work from the very last text sent) so I just thought I'd put everything in to be safe!!!  So send me your most up to date up to date copy when you've made your very minor adjustments!  Strange and morbid hmmm…and I thought I'd learnt to do comedy!!!  Not really.  'Blow goats' is probably what you think… – fellatio with a goat!!!! – it's very insulting and crude.  'Rave for the PF': rave as in rave parties and also like a huge cheer like 'Go mad for the PF' (but very slangy)  PF I've no idea – it's a local reference and can be translated PF!!!!  You are very clever – I couldn't begin to deal with translation like this in any of the bits of foreign languages I know.

*to Marko*
I sent you a postcard today…and now here's all my answers to the translation questions. Very late I know but now Copenhagen is rearing an autumn head, I thought I'd better answer those very interesting questions of yours.

*p107:* There is nothing special about 'The Billy Goats Gruff'. It's simply a picture in relief on the back of the fire showing the goats, the bridge and the troll – sometimes wood burning stoves have these reliefs inside and they are lit up when the fire is burning. Everyone in England would not know it!

    Pace Egg. Pace Egg is 'Paschal Egg' or 'Easter Egg', except it actually doesn't have the same sweet connotations as an Easter egg. It's an old seasonal festival in the north of England to do with ploughing the land which takes place around Easter/Spring time, and when plays are performed in the streets by strange characters which look back to earth rites, one of whom may distribute coloured chickens' eggs from a basket to the crowd. I used the actual basket when playing the character who gives out the eggs! There is nothing special about the basket – it's a simple willow basket. Maybe you need to translate it as 'dark willow basket or 'basket of woven willow' – something like that. I can't see how you are going to get the connotations of 'Pace Egg', which is pretty obscure in English let alone Finnish.

*p113:* 'Hair straighteners' (particularly the make GHD) are still very popular with young women here.

'Screwed up revision about the liver': Rowan has been revising for her Biology exam (GCSE – the final exam you take at age 16 in England). She has been doing human biology, looking at the functions of the liver, and making pencil notes. When she has finished the revision, she has crumpled up the piece of paper in a ball, thrown it towards the rubbish bin, and missed – so it's a screwed up ball on the floor.

*p115:* 'a riddle'. This must be VERY difficult to translate. The curve is literally the shape of the dolphin's back, as it's rising out of the water. It appears to just touch (nudge) the white foam at the top of the wave. I'm imagining the dolphin going across the path of the wave and then disappearing back into the sea before the wave falls, while just touching the spume (another English word for the foam at the top of the wave) – so it's a very brief appearance. We also say 'the crest of the wave' for the top of the wave. I'm looking down from the edge of a steep, sheer granite cliff into the rough sea below, in West Cornwall – which is very rugged, wild landscape. So the drop is 'fall'. I'm pretty sure that the 'curve' I saw in the water was a dolphin so I run back along the cliff paths to my house to tell my family. 'Tufts' is not usually used about waves but about hair or fur, so it's a reference back to the hair straighteners etc. Isn't poetry complicated?! I'd no idea all these layers were there until I tried to answer your questions. There's obviously a word play in 'tidings' too, which literally means 'news' but I'm referring back to the sea tides as well. 'Tidings' is quite a formal, literary word in English and appears in the words of a Christmas carol: Gabriel the angel brings Mary 'tidings of great joy'. 'Wonder-full', as you know, is an invention and a play on the original word so I don't know what you can do with this, but I'm sure what you've done will be fine! It should sound much heavier than 'wonderful'.

Yes stanzas are really called stanzas – it seems more common than 'verses' these days. Don't know why.

*p117:* I'm not sure the dolpin-like creature is identified with Matthew's daughter, though there is a connotation of this. In some way, his daughter is sending a message through the dolphin-like creature but she herself isn't the creature. Because the dolphin is a special token for Rowan, this is how the voice appears to Matthew. I'm not sure I've quite worked this out. I think the energy of the violent death has somehow been translated into the dolphin-like creature, as ghosts inhabit chests of drawers and wardrobes, moving them about – as well as appearing in more human forms.

Sorry you had to descend into the underworld of English personal pronouns. You may be able to deal with it more like this:

He can't see it but he hears it
sounding like an old woman
grunting beneath his window

instead of

He can't see her but he hears her:
she sounds like an old woman
grunting beneath his window.

and

He hears a sigh,
stands there, listens.
The dolphin's calling from higher up.

instead of

He hears the dolphin sigh,
stands there, listens,
till she calls from higher up.

Of course, the first version doesn't scan in English but it avoids using 'she' for the dolphin and I only use 'she' for the dolphin on these two occasions in the poem. 'Her' you presumably translate as 'it'.

YES, I hope this makes things clearer in the Finnish and I think you're right to make a clear distinction between daughter and dolphin in the Finnish. There's actually a fairly clear distinction between the two in my head but I'm finding it quite hard to explain.

*p123:* 'Fen church' because in England there is the region called 'The Fens', and it's this I'm referring to, though there are obviously fens outside this region as well. The churches are usually on islands of more stable higher ground in the Fens and you can see them from a long way away, like Ely cathedral. A Rayburn is the brand name of a kind of slow burning stove which keeps going all through the day and night, heating the water, keeping the kitchen warm and you can use the top for cooking on. Great things! When I was growing up, we had one in our kitchen. I don't know about Finnish letters for the musical scale (though I do enjoy Sibelius and do really play Finnish polkas!). The first note of the piece (Debussy's 'Syrinx') is definitely B flat in English, which is not the same note as A (the note below B flat).

Phew! About the introductory sentences you talk about I'm not sure. Is your concern to do with the lighter tone used for these? What do other people think? (e.g. Carita, Ralf). The first one could simply be, 'The watery tale begins...' I still think I need something here to signify that the actual story is beginning. Similarly, the end piece could simply say 'There are many more writings yet to be written and yet to be read...' What do you think now? (seven weeks later!). I like the fact that I'm suggesting the narrative of the rest of the story, which I haven't written yet.

## Ralf and Steve

*Från: Ralf*
*Till: Steve*
I turned 40 just before Christmas – a bit too much for my liking. Ulla gave me a fabulous gift: a gramophone, actually a jukebox, from the late 1920's, plays 78's of course. I probably won't use it very often because those old acoustic gramophones with heavy pick-ups are so tough on the records (I have a couple of 1950's 78 rpm gramophones with a lighter electronic pick-ups as well) but it's a beautiful piece of equipment. I played some original Bessie Smith 78's last night and the sound was wonderful, so genuine and rich compared to the tinny sound you get when playing her on CD. I got needles from a music shop in Jakobstad, about 100 kilometres north of Vasa. It's a wonderful place – the owner hasn't renewed stock since the early 1970's and some of the stuff, most of it unused, dates back to the 1940's. He hardly sells anything – the shop's just like a time capsule – surreal, scary almost.

*From: Steve*
*To: Ralf*
Just dug our lava lamp out of the attic. I found in Spain when working alone long hours that they created a sense of movement in static space. Mind you, you didn't have to put your coat on to go out on the balcony there – here we've got the tail end of that storm we flew into Vaasa on last year.

*Från: Ralf*
*Till: Steve*
Lava lamps are nice. It's a pity they came back into fashion, though. I liked it when they were just a half-forgotten 60's fad. They were invented in 1963, just like me.

We've had too much work and too little play up here in the north in recent months, but the good news is that there's a whiff of spring in the air. Or was. There's actually a cold sleety wind today. I miss the view we had in our old flat, the park, the water. Here there's just a bit of sky and the yellow wall of the old diesel engine factory. In a way it's rather aesthetic, but it's too zen for me at the moment, I could do with some variety. More spaciousness.

*From: Steve*
*To: Ralf*
Well, here at my desk the view is pure suburbia, if I stand on a chair and lean out I can see hills. To one side the houses are very ugly. The only saving grace is the gardens. If I think about suburbia too much I begin to feel claustrophobic so I'll stop.

*Från: Ralf*
*Till: Steve*
Back from the flea market, bought 5 CD's for a euro each. Pretty good stuff too. Had to get out for a while, been sitting in front of the computer all day, so I jumped on my bicycle and rode off. The weather is almost too warm, +25 C, in early May. Makes people crazy – all this pressure that has been building up inside during the winter. Naked skin everywhere suddenly. You can tell everyone's full of expectations, most of which will be thwarted during the summer and then they'll be ready for the sobering melancholy of autumn. I'd prefer to

be permanently drunk with melancholy – good way of avoiding disappointment.

*From: Steve*
*To: Carita*
*CC: Ralf*
Many thanks for your translation of 'Aire', wonderful, I am just about to get on a train, people will be wondering who is doing the Bergman voice over impression in the corner of the carriage I just can't help reading it out aloud.

*Från: Ralf*
*Till: Steve*
I read your piece several times last week. Actually I read it quickly in Stockholm waiting for the plane to Vasa, but I wasn't properly focused then. I had another go last Friday when, after teaching in the morning, I spent most of day in a number of cafés reading. I haven't really done that before – it's too close to the stereotype of the wanna be local bard – but I've noticed that I actually like to sit and read in public places, I'm able to concentrate the way I want to, when I'm surrounded by the noise and buzz of conversation and clatter of cups.

*From: Steve*
*To: Ralf*
Walking to the restaurant this lunchtime, I was thinking how you and I always talk about the weather, how it has come to frame and connect our relationship. I can't look at a weather map, or satellite image or watch/listen to a weather forecast now without checking what its doing up in that little bump on the side of Finland. In Gandia I get Sky European forecasts, the edges of their map are Vasa and Tunisia.

*Från: Ralf*
*Till: Steve*
I've now translated my piece and I'm enclosing it. There might be bits/passages that sound odd, but sometimes it's intentional – I use quirky syntax and ambiguous references in the Swedish original at some points – but there might of course also be constructions that don't work or don't sound good in English. I'm very grateful for any comments.

*Från: Ralf*
*Till: Steve*
I have revised my text and it's ready except for one word that's still causing me problems. I've removed 'greasily' but it's proved difficult to find an alternative. Can you help me out? The last version is the neatest, but it's not supposed to be like that, it's supposed to be a bit crammed, overloaded, mannerist, slightly pornographic even, sort of undermining the romanticism of the poem.

*From: Steve*
*To: Ralf*
The watering horses conundrum might be interesting to have the others feed back on, there is an oscillation in English but it is very weak because watering a horse is so specifically giving it drink – maybe Adam might have a wonderful old English word or even Romany word that more fully means both drenching and giving a drink.

The Whernside quotation made me laugh, it's true but probably written by a Lancastrian, if said by a

Yorkshire person it would be the finest biggest 'ill in t'world.

Snow mobiles – I get the picture absolutely, and it should be handlebars, in fact I've just been on a snow mobile parts website and they call them handlebars (a whole new world), it is good too because for me a snow mobile was a bigger thing you sat inside (I used to have a Dinky one) so this clarifies it is more of a scooter too.

As for the *Interland* website, the stats for August show we had about 40 serious visitors, ie. People who stayed and looked around and not crawlers or people tapping strange things into search engines – 'Sudan kidnappings', 'all you can eats signs', 'her headache motorway' – and not so strange – 'Adam Strickson', 'Carita San Francisco' – and those who I should imagine were pretty disappointed to get us – 'double action sexi', 'creamy tugs', 'housewife humps her pillow'!

*Från: Ralf*
*Till: Steve*
*CC: Adam, Carita, Kath, Marko*
I'm a bit late as always. It's no excuse, but I was born late in the year, in the evening. It was dark, the wind howled out on the snowy fields. And then I contracted pneumonia. The final version of my piece should be in your mail boxes soon.

*From: Steve*
*Till: Ralf*
This morning Ella May woke up and said, Daddy, what are solids? Tonight she told me that tomorrow winter starts and she likes winter best because it will snow, and she asked me how it snowed so we got to talking about how ice was solid water and snow was little bits of ice and I was thinking of you when out of the blue Ella asks, 'Is it snowing at Ralf and Ulla's house?'

It feels like winter [English winter] starting, but really it's autumn.

**Steve Dearden**'s short stories have been published in magazines in England, Finland and Australia and he was Writer in Residence at Bluewater Shopping Centre in Kent as part of Architexts. He runs The Writing Squad, a development programme for writers aged 16-20 in Yorkshire and produced Foundland, an exchange between UK and Canadian writers. www.stevedearden.com

**Kath McKay** was born in Liverpool, studied in Belfast and London and lives in Leeds. Publications include *Waiting for the Morning* (The Women's Press, 1991) and *Anyone Left Standing* (Smith/Doorstop 1998). Her short stories and poetry appear in magazines, anthologies and have been broadcast. She taught adults creative writing 1987-2004. She has written on the swimming pools of Leeds, regeneration in East Hull, and teeth (collaborating with a visual artist). Until spring 2006 she was an online mentor for Crossing Borders, working with writers in Africa.

**Ralf Andtbacka** was born in Kronoby north of Vasa. He is a poet and critic, passionate about English and American poetry. From 2000 to 2005 he was Lead Artist in Literature for the Ostrobothnian Arts Commission and Director of the Vaasa Littfest. He has published four collections including *Café Sjöjungfrun* (1999) and *En fisk som man kan se* (2004).

**Carita Nyström**, born 1940 in Vasa, studied literature in Helsinki and Copenhagen. Having worked at Helsinki university and Finnish radio for a number of years she moved back to Ostrobothnia in the early eighties. Since 1975 she has published ten books of poetry and prose, As 'regional guiding artist' for literature in Ostrobothnia (1991-93) she initiated a Writer's School. Since 1995 she has also worked with writing workshops for children, visiting schools to talk about the adventure of reading and writing.

**Adam Strickson** is a playwright, poet and occasional visual artist, who lives in a shambling Victorian house on a very steep hill near Huddersfield. His father is a classical musician and his grandfather was a sailor.

For thirteen years, he was director of Chol Theatre, the pioneering inter-cultural company based in Batley, West Yorkshire. He travelled to Bangladesh, India, Denmark and Poland working for the company. The name 'Chol' means 'the sound of water lapping against the side of a boat' or 'Get going!' in Bengali. He is now a freelance writer. His first poetry collection, *An Indian Rug Surprised by Snow*, was published by Wrecking Ball Press in 2005, when he was also poet-in-residence at Ilkley Literature Festival.

**Marko Hautala**'s first novel *Kirottu maa* (*Cursed Earth*) was published in 2002. Before and after that he has published short stories and poetry in different Finnish magazines and anthologies. In addition he teaches creative writing, writes book reviews for the newspaper *Pohjalainen* and works on his doctoral thesis on William Blake's notion of the subversive imagination and the 'unrational'.